YOUR GUIDE to the
Most *Popular* Features
of the **US National Parks**

Stefanie Payne

ADAMS MEDIA
NEW YORK   LONDON   TORONTO   SYDNEY   NEW DELHI

Adams Media
An Imprint of Simon & Schuster, Inc.
100 Technology Center Drive
Stoughton, Massachusetts 02072

First Adams Media hardcover edition
December 2022

ADAMS MEDIA and colophon are
trademarks of Simon & Schuster.

For information about special discounts
for bulk purchases, please contact
Simon & Schuster Special Sales at
1-866-506-1949 or
business@simonandschuster.com.

The Simon & Schuster Speakers Bureau
can bring authors to your live event. For
more information or to book an event
contact the Simon & Schuster Speakers
Bureau at 1-866-248-3049 or visit our
website at www.simonspeakers.com.

Interior design by Colleen Cunningham
Interior illustrations by Alaya Howard
Interior images © Getty Images/Kateryna
Novokhatnia; 123RF/Adrian Laschi

Manufactured in the United States of
America

1 2022

Library of Congress Cataloging-in-
Publication Data
Names: Payne, Stefanie, author.
Title: 100 things to see in the national
parks / Stefanie Payne.
Other titles: One hundred things to see in
the National Parks
Description: Stoughton, Massachusetts:
Adams Media, [2022] |
Includes index.
Identifiers: LCCN 2022038751 | ISBN
9781507219980 (hc) | ISBN 9781507219997
(ebook)
Subjects: LCSH: National parks and
reserves--United States--Guidebooks.
Classification: LCC E160 .P39 2022 | DDC
333.78160973--dc23/eng/20220830
LC record available at
https://lccn.loc.gov/2022038751

ISBN 978-1-5072-1998-0
ISBN 978-1-5072-1999-7 (ebook)

Dedication

For the US Department of the Interior, the US National Park Service, and to the rangers and all who work there—thank you for preserving our public lands and for teaching, inspiring, and helping visitors have safer and more meaningful journeys in America's national parks.

To dedicated national park explorers, who pour their experiences onto the pages of books, websites, and social media platforms: Your wisdom, guidance, and infectious enthusiasm illuminate pathways to new experiences that enhance the beauty in our lives.

And to my beloved husband, father, siblings, and friends—for being so very patient with me while I'm on deadline! Thank you for loving me, and for supporting me in all of my quests to explore our wild and wonderful world.

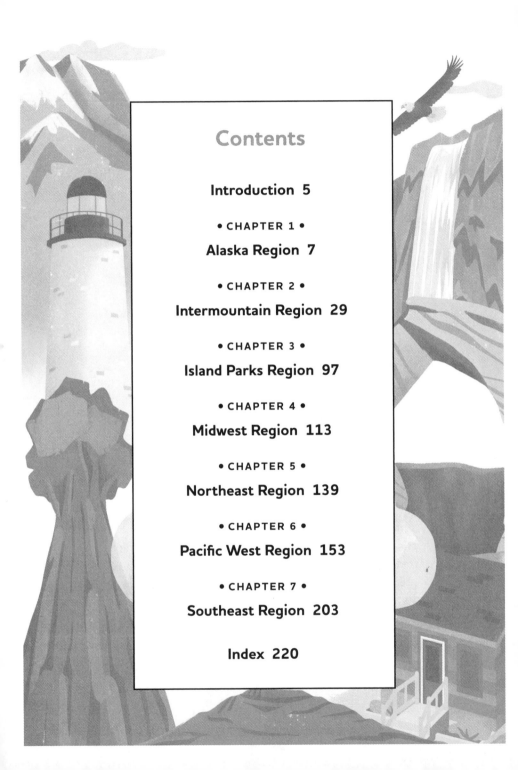

Contents

Introduction

Would you like to:

Touch the world's oldest, tallest, and largest trees?
Experience the hottest place on Earth?
Journey to North America's highest peak?
Explore the longest mapped cave system in the world?

You can see all this and more in America's national parks. There are sixty-three national parks in the United States—spanning eighty-five million acres—and each has distinct qualities that have captured the hearts of visitors from all over the world. Every park has can't-miss destinations—places that, if you left the park without seeing, you'd regret missing out. *100 Things to See in the National Parks* is a collection of these celebrated landmarks, historical places, breathtaking natural settings, and fascinating points of interest found in America's most treasured lands. While must-see lists are largely subjective, the locations highlighted here have astonished viewers for centuries and have served as sacred landmarks for millennia to native communities.

In these pages you'll learn about lesser-known spots as well, such as rare arctic sand dunes, colorful volcanoes decorated by endangered plants that glitter like jewels, and scenic byways that carve through remote wilderness you might otherwise have never seen. This book will tell you how and where to find such spots—and will inspire you to want to go!

Each entry lists the location of the featured attraction in the park, the best times to visit it, and how to get there. You'll also find a Must-See Guide that goes into more depth about what the attraction is, why it is important, and anything you will need to know to plan your trip or enjoy this location.

As you journey through this book and ponder your next must-see destinations, you will learn more about each of the national parks and what makes them so special. Whether you've visited some of the parks before or are on a new journey of discovery, you'll love exploring these unique and awe-inspiring places. Adventure awaits!

AK

CHAPTER 1

Alaska Region

AK

Denali Park Road

Your Must-See Guide

With only one established road leading into a magnificent river-strewn landscape, you can understand what makes Denali Park Road so important in terms of seeing the enchanting wilderness that enfolds this national park. It is ninety-two miles long (one way), and private vehicles are permitted to travel only the first fifteen miles of paved roadway to the Savage River area, where you can set up and stay awhile at the designated park campground; venture onward to finish your guided park road excursion; or hop off the bus and explore on your own by foot.

The remaining seventy-seven miles of unpaved road beyond that point must be experienced aboard a concessioner-operated tour/shuttle bus that offers daily trips to the road's rugged end at Kantishna—once a gold mining town and now a coveted area to stay in the remote wilderness.

Hopping onto narrated or non-narrated transit bus tours allows for immersive experiences, with several scheduled stops at various points of interest (for example, the Toklat River and the Eielson Visitor Center), as well as unscheduled stops when wildlife unexpectedly appears, which is undoubtedly a highlight of the journey.

Traveling through four mountain passes, sprawling views of spruce forests and untrammeled landscapes spread out in the distance. With every mile gained, the mammoth Denali peak comes closer into view as you near the end of the road. Just a short walk from Wonder Lake at mile

PLAN AHEAD AND MONITOR CONDITIONS

Due to the ever-changing environment and unpredictable weather systems in interior Alaska, always check the official website for Denali at www.nps.gov/dena for updates related to road, trail, and area closures. Because of the park's popularity, you'll want to check on permit requirements and reservations during planning and upon arrival.

marker 85 (markers follow miles of road) sits Reflection Pond, where on a clear day you can capture a mirror view of Denali and the Alaska Range.

Park Snapshot

Denali is mostly known for its wild scenery, braided rivers, abundant wildlife populations, and massive glacier-capped mountains that tower overhead. The park was initially established to protect Dall sheep before extending protections to include caribou, wolf, moose, and grizzly bears—a true prize if you witness all five of them all in one trip! Adventurers love the challenging terrain that makes for unforgettable hiking and backpacking expeditions. There are plenty of experiences for visitors of all ages and all levels of skill and wilderness knowledge. Denali is the only national park with working sled dogs, inviting guests each year to mush alongside them during popular demonstrations hosted by the National Park Service (NPS). It is a haven for endemic and migratory birds, beckoning bird-watchers keen to add to their life lists. You can get a bird's-eye view as well by hopping on a "flightseeing" tour to soar above the six-million-acre landscape.

• WHAT •

The only established roadway in Denali National Park and Preserve.

• WHERE •

On the northeast side of the park, starting at the park entrance.

• WHEN TO VISIT •

May through September, when weather is favorable, and the midnight sun illuminates the landscape at almost all hours of the day and night. There are off-season travel opportunities year-round, though fewer services and activities will be available during these times.

• HOW TO GET THERE •

The George Parks Highway (Alaska 3) is the only connecter between Denali and Alaska's two largest cities: Anchorage is two hundred and thirty-seven miles to the south, and Fairbanks is one hundred and twenty-five miles to the north. The national park entrance is located at mile 237, and from there, you can't miss the entrance to Denali Park Road.

AK

Denali Mountain

Your Must-See Guide

Standing at 20,310 feet above sea level, Denali towers over the rugged wilderness of interior Alaska. It is so high and large that it creates its own weather systems that frequently shroud it from view, though it is technically visible anywhere in central and south-central Alaska. The Athabascan name *Denali* translates as "The High One" or "The Great One" and was restored as the official park name in 2016, effectively retiring Mount McKinley. Between its sacred standing among Native Alaskans, its mountaineering history and present-day culture, and the sheer beauty of contoured glaciers that rise high above the area—it is no wonder that Denali is a must-see!

It is one of the most isolated peaks on Earth and one of the world's largest massifs (a compact grouping of mountains). The forever-snowcapped mountain makes the tundra-blanketed slopes of the region look softer and greener. The ice at the top—an area dipping to negative 75°F during the winter—tells the story of the glacier age, and now the modern age of glacier melt, which sends water to flow through the region, feeding wildlife and providing passageways from one area of the landscape to the next. From the mountain of Denali, it all flows downstream. Whether you are seeing it reflected in clear lakes, standing above the landscape, or taking it in from the air on a flightseeing tour—the pinnacle of the national park is sure to take your breath away!

A DIFFICULT JOURNEY

With its steep vertical climbs and harsh weather, Denali is considered one of the most difficult mountains on Earth to climb. Nevertheless, hundreds of people try each year. In 1906, Frederick Cook claimed to be the first person to have reached the top, but that was later proved to be false. In reality, the first climbers to reach the peak were Hudson Stuck, Harry Karstens, and their team in 1913.

Denali Mountain is one of the most isolated peaks on Earth and one of the world's largest compact grouping of mountains. The forever-snowcapped mountain makes the tundra-blanketed slopes of the region look softer and greener.

• WHAT •

North America's tallest mountain.

• WHERE •

In the south-central area of the park.

• WHEN TO VISIT •

Late May through mid-September is high season, when the days are warm and long—and when you have the best chance of seeing Denali's peak. Cloud cover hides the high area of Denali 70 percent of the time, so consider yourself lucky if you can catch a glimpse of it during your time there.

• HOW TO GET THERE •

Denali is a coveted area for mountaineers, and how you get there will depend on your exploration goals. To see the legendary peak—which you can do from many areas in Alaska—head to the park's neighboring town of Talkeetna, Denali State Park, and to the end of Denali Park Road. To experience its terrain on a mountaineering or climbing expedition, contact the NPS ranger staff at the park's Walter Harper Talkeetna Ranger Station for advice and to obtain information on permitting and planning.

AK

Arrigetch Peaks

Your Must-See Guide

Want to see a wild and beautiful mountainous landscape in the only region where you can find US national parks located above the Arctic Circle? If that is a yes, then be sure not to miss the Arrigetch Peaks, which are among the most prominent geological features in the Gates of the Arctic. *Arrigetch* translates in Iñupiat as "fingers of the hand extended," and these peaks serve as a recognizable landmark to the Native Alaskan Nunamiut people. The fingers, or peaks, really do extend, reaching to the sky and cascading water from their glacier-formed tops into alpine lakes and rivers that flow across delicate tundra and into boreal forests.

If this is not your primary destination in the park, you are still likely to catch glimpses of the formation as you fly into Gates. If a flyby isn't enough, have no fear—there are many private air charter companies that offer flightseeing adventures that soar above the granite pinnacles and glacial valleys that sprawl out from their base.

The Arrigetch Peaks and surrounding areas appeal to backpackers, technical climbers, and mountaineers who prize remote and hard-to-get-to places wherever they can find them. Be certain to check out the official National Park Service website for Gates at www.nps.gov/gaar before your visit. Experience in the backcountry is a must if you plan to guide your own adventure. If you are more comfortable heading

BE AWARE THAT YOU ARE ON YOUR OWN

Gates is a premier wilderness park, and with that comes solitude—and solitude here guarantees that you are essentially on your own. There are no services or communications signals, and oftentimes trips need to be extended or shortened if pilots cannot fly due to unexpected weather conditions. Planning and preparation are key.

into the remote area with a guided group, there are several seasoned operators in the area who know the terrain, history, ethical considerations, and permit requirements.

Park Snapshot

If you want to experience unadulterated wilderness far from the general buzz of humanity, this is the park for you. Gates is listed as one of the top three least visited parks year after year, primarily because of its remote location. The diverse ecosystem is home to an array of natural features—from glacier-carved mountains to forests and alpine tundra. There are six designated Wild and Scenic Rivers flowing through the park, providing passage to humans and wildlife. Subsistence communities in the region continue to hunt the land and fish the waters as they have for millennia. Today, visitors head out on rafting adventures, where they can see grizzly bears, musk ox, caribou, and moose on the riverbanks peeking through the trees. The park has no roads, no established campgrounds or designated trails, and no services—it is just you, your gear, and your travel companions in almost perfectly pure wilderness.

• WHAT •

A collection of dramatic granite spires in the Endicott Mountains in northern Alaska's central Brooks Range.

• WHERE •

In the remote southwest area of the national park.

• WHEN TO VISIT •

Weather is warmest from mid-June through September. The park lies in the arctic and subarctic climate zone, and weather can change unexpectedly any time of year. Check conditions before you travel.

• HOW TO GET THERE •

Most recreational visitors travel to the area by way of chartered aircraft from Fairbanks or from the small towns of Bettles or Coldfoot outside the southeastern edge of the park. Check with air taxi companies for drop locations if going on your own. If you're exploring with a tour group, your outfitter likely has transit covered.

AK

Glacier Bay Basin

Your Must-See Guide

Glacier Bay—among the largest UNESCO-protected biosphere in the world—is surrounded by rugged mountains and dense forests in a land where the native Huna Tlingit preserve a subsistence lifestyle that maintains a connection to their past ancestors. The soul of this park lies in the water, where glaciers have spilled out for thousands of years to feed the icy waterways that provide a happy home for aquatic wildlife and birdlife.

Pushing off from dedicated areas of Bartlett Cove, you can start your guided or solo paddling excursions to explore the marine habitat where humpback whales, sea otters, and a variety of other species glide alongside you as you head deeper into the bay. Beneath your watercraft, large populations of fish sustain marine life, while along rocky shorelines nearby, wolves and bears feed on tidal delicacies.

The Glacier Bay Tour Boat operated by the National Park Service is a fun and immersive way to spend a day. Careening through Bartlett Cove and Glacier Bay, a narrator on daylong outings teaches visitors about the ecosystem and people of the area while pausing for wildlife sightings along the way. Select cruises lead to famed landmarks like Margerie Glacier—an actively calving glacier where booming echoes of glacial ice hitting the water command full attention.

When your daily summer adventures conclude, the fabled midnight sun blends fun-filled days into long summer nights, allowing

WHERE TO STAY IN GLACIER BAY

There are a small number of places to stay if exploring Glacier Bay independently of a cruise ship. Bartlett Cove Campground and Glacier Bay Lodge and Tours are two options in the national park, and there are a handful of locally operated accommodations in the nearby town of Gustavus.

your adventure to extend as you relax in the majestic surroundings.

Park Snapshot

In Glacier Bay, travelers come from all over the world to watch humpback whales breach and orcas porpoise the surface waters, while bald eagles soar overhead as commonly as gulls do in most marinas in contiguous North America. The waters protect rich populations of salmon, halibut, and other large species of fish that entice sport anglers keen on dropping a line in the cold Alaskan waters (an activity that is allowed within the national park boundary when adhering to recreational fishing regulations).

The land-based areas surrounding Glacier Bay are not to be ignored. Trails into conifer forests allow peaceful wanders in areas where you are almost certain to see some form of wildlife along the way.

Contrasting the natural experience is an important cultural history to explore honoring Native Alaskan communities that are preserved in artifacts, totems, natural artwork, and narratives that are storied by indigenous peopke of the region and the National Park Service.

• WHAT •

A tidewater glacier-carved bay surrounded by unspoiled Alaskan wilderness where marine life is abundant.

• WHERE •

In the southeast area of the national park, on the Gulf of Alaska and the Icy Strait.

• WHEN TO VISIT •

May through September is high season in Glacier Bay, when the weather is warmest and aquatic animals are migrating through the area.

• HOW TO GET THERE •

There are two ways to get to Glacier Bay: You can arrive via chartered boat or cruise ship, or you can drive from the small town of Gustavus located ten miles from the national park visitor center. Gustavus is accessible by bush flight via Anchorage (and other small towns) or by car traveling in from the Yukon Territory.

AK

Brooks Falls

Your Must-See Guide

While Katmai National Park and Preserve sprawls across four million acres of pristine wilderness, the scene at Brooks Falls is by far the most famous spot in the park—thanks in large part to the National Park Service bear cams positioned near the falls that transmit the scene to the world, as well as through the work of photographers and videographers who have captured epic action scenes of bears doing their annual dance for food each summer. At any of the three viewing platforms at Brooks Camp,

CONSIDER HIRING A GUIDE

Enlisting a guided outfitter is a smart idea if you plan to explore beyond Brooks Camp. You will learn more about the area with increased safety by traveling with pros who understand the region, know how to respond to unpredictable weather, cross impassable areas, and stay safe around wildlife.

you can watch grizzly bears weighing up to one thousand pounds (along with slightly smaller mama bears and their cubs) paw sockeye salmon as the schools make their way to their spawning grounds upstream.

Because of the popularity of this spot and for the safety of the bear populations, there is limited access to Brooks Falls. You can either stay in concessionaire-operated accommodations via a lottery system or, if you are up for camping in bear country, pitch a tent at a primitive campground. Once in the park, your days will mostly be spent on the viewing platforms. You can also enjoy a number of small hikes on established trails and enjoy peaceful forests and the lakeshore—all areas where bear activity is a regular occurrence. The National Park Service offers daily educational programs, as well as day trips to the Valley of Ten Thousand Smokes twenty-three miles from camp— where you can explore the remnants left by the eruption of the Novarupta volcano.

Park Snapshot

Katmai National Park and Preserve was originally established to protect the Valley of Ten Thousand Smokes. Today, it is best known for its large populations of massive brown bears who steal the show every year at Brooks Falls. Katmai's protected area is enormous, and wildlife thrives throughout the park thanks to food sources in the forests and on waterways that teem with calorie-rich fish and shellfish found in rivers and lakes and onshore. The salmon that sustain bears through hibernation during long Alaska winters, along with abundant schools of rainbow trout and arctic char, attract sport fishers whom you might see wading through the rivers with a line in hand. Katmai serves up incredible backcountry excursions as well, including paddling adventures along extensive coastlines and wilderness backpacking trips. Flightseeing tours that soar above the roadless geography can be seen overhead from any of these vantage points.

• WHAT •

A legendary viewing location of Alaskan brown bears feeding on sockeye salmon.

• WHERE •

On the Brooks River, one and a half miles between Brooks Lake and Naknek Lake.

• WHEN TO VISIT •

While bears are active from June through September, the best times for bear viewing at Brooks are in July and September, when salmon populations are the most concentrated, both during spawn and at the end of their life cycle.

• HOW TO GET THERE •

The only way to get to Naknek Lake near Brooks Falls is by floatplane from the Alaska town of King Salmon, which can be reached by a commercial flight from Anchorage. You can also get to Brooks Camp by powerboats pushing off from the villages of Naknek and King Salmon.

Valley of Ten Thousand Smokes

AK

Your Must-See Guide

The Valley of Ten Thousand Smokes is where the world's largest and most catastrophic volcanic eruption during the twentieth century occurred. In 1912, the later-named Novarupta volcano sent ash and pumice sky-high for nearly three days before it rushed into the Ukak River Valley, transforming forty square miles of wilderness landscape into a barren wasteland. Today, the area is decorated by colorful volcanic ash deposits, braided rivers, and glacier-filled mountains rising overhead. A trip there makes one ponder the turbulent history that resides in what now is pure wildness.

There are no established trails here, though there are several popular hiking areas including Baked Mountain, Katmai Pass and the Trident Lava Flows, and the Mount Katmai caldera. Rivers and streams that run through the area punctuate a beautiful scene and unusual landscape. Special care should be taken while crossing, as the rivers are swift and the volcanic ash can make for treacherous conditions.

The Buttress Range is a popular place to set up camp beneath starry skies. Plywood shelters built by the United States Geological Survey (USGS) known as "Baked Mountain Huts" were once a popular temporary dwelling option for backcountry backpackers, but they were destroyed by a storm in 2018 and are no longer safe to use.

BRING PLENTY OF WATER

The Valley of Ten Thousand Smokes is one of the few places in Alaska where drinking water is scarce. Especially in the month of August, when the temperatures are generally at their highest, it is suggested that you bring plenty of water. Several of the streams in the valley have large amounts of silt, pumice, and sand, which can clog water filters. When you do encounter drinkable water in the Valley, drink up and store some for later.

An easy (in Alaska terms) entrance point is from Brooks Camp located twenty-three miles away, where day-trippers can head out to explore and return at nightfall if staying at Brooks Lodge or the Brooks primitive campsite. Backpackers heading into the area can arrange for drop-offs and pickups days later.

The area around Valley of Ten Thousand Smokes is decorated by colorful volcanic ash deposits, braided rivers, and glacier-filled mountains rising overhead.

• WHAT •

An area impacted by the largest volcanic eruption of the twentieth century and a prime destination for day trips and backcountry adventures.

• WHERE •

In the south-central area of the park.

• WHEN TO VISIT •

Trips operate from June through October, though July and August usually have the warmest weather. It's cooler here than at Brooks Falls, and weather can change without notice, so bring layers and appropriate rain gear.

• HOW TO GET THERE •

Fly a commercial aircraft from Anchorage or the town of King Salmon to Naknek Lake near Brooks Falls. Concessionaire-operated buses depart once a day from Brooks during high season. Private charter companies can drop you directly at the Valley of Ten Thousand Smokes.

Kenai Fjords by Boat Cruise

AK

Your Must-See Guide

Exploring coastal Alaska is a one-of-a-kind experience, and day trips into the Kenai Fjords are made easy, as boat cruises operate regularly during high season through national park–operated excursions pushing off from the Seward waterfront.

On half- or full-day sea voyages, you will navigate through glacier-carved landmasses jutting out from the water while taking in stunning views of ice-capped mountains and trees that hug the sea the entire way. On half-day tours in Resurrection Bay, spectacular scenery is met by frequent sightings of birds and sea animals including stellar

A CRUISE FOR EVERYONE

Kenai Fjords offers many types of boat cruises. Some cruises cater to bird-watchers, some to those looking to get the perfect pictures, and some that are family friendly. Do some research and find the type of cruise that suits your needs best.

sea lions, sea otters, porpoises, bald eagles, and colorful puffins whose nesting grounds nestle on the moss-draped sea stacks.

Venturing out on a full-day tour, you will see a more expansive ecosystem unfold as you coast to active tidewater glaciers (Holgate and Aialik Glaciers) in Aialik Bay. This area has some of the best whale watching in Alaska, with orca, humpback, gray, fin, and minke whales all migrating through the area every summer. The broader waterways are also home to seabird rookeries and nesting grounds. There is nothing cooler than seeing a humpback breach or puffins nesting on fjords!

Wildlife sightings vary by species, and there are certain months and weeks to get the best look at each kind, so do some research before you plan your trip to identify your sighting priorities.

Ship captains and naturalists onboard narrate the tours while helping to spot animals, identify scenic landmarks, and answer questions along the way so you learn about all you are seeing.

Park Snapshot

Its easy-to-get-to location just under one hundred and twenty-five miles from Alaska's capital in Anchorage makes Kenai Fjords one of the most accessible parks in Alaska and one of the few you can drive to in just a few hours from a major city.

Recreational travelers love it because there is great camping both in the park and in the neighboring community of Seward. As you travel farther from the marine shores and deeper into the park, outings large and small take shape in the forests, on mountains, and on glaciers that flow out to sea where the unimpaired marine environment couldn't be livelier!

The mile-high Harding Icefield in the Kenai Mountains is the centerpiece of the park, covering half its area. Harding is the largest icefield in the United States and can be seen on a flightseeing tour or along the Harding Icefield Trail if you are up for an ice-hiking adventure.

• WHAT •

Scenic cruises of various types that lead to some of the greatest land- and sea-based features of the national park—from marine life to rare birds to glacier-carved fjords that enfold the waterways.

• WHERE •

Starting in the northeast area of the park; traveling southeast to areas along the coastline (depending on the type of tour you take).

• WHEN TO VISIT •

Tours operate most frequently from May through early October during prime Alaska tourist season.

• HOW TO GET THERE •

Arrive at the town of Seward by car or boat and head to the national park visitor center to make arrangements for your tour. You can also book trips in advance through the National Park Service website for Kenai Fjords at www.nps.gov/kefj.

AK

Great Kobuk Sand Dunes

Your Must-See Guide

There are very few dune fields on Earth like the Great Kobuk Sand Dunes. They are located entirely above the Arctic Circle and are the largest active dunes at high latitude, formed over the course of millions of years by glacier movement. While the incredibly pure landscape of powdered sand idles beneath your feet, geological wonders like crystalized jade and schist are scattered throughout the dunes indiscriminately. Lush, delicate wildflowers and arctic grasses surface during the late spring and summer months, lending colorful bursts and interesting textures onto the golden formations.

To step foot onto the sand dunes lends an instant feeling of being one of the only people to ever walk there apart from Native Alaskans and large herds of wildlife. The park is completely wild and nearly devoid of human impact. In fact, so few visitors travel there, seeing a footprint in the sand would be highly unusual, as strong northern winds constantly resurface the landscape by layering decorated patterns across the drifts. What you are more likely to see are animal tracks left by grizzly bears, wolves, and caribou that roam the region.

The Great Kobuk Sand Dunes are the largest of three dune fields in the national park and are the most accessible and arguably the grandest—standing one hundred miles high across twenty-five square miles. There are no established trails, so you can blaze your own path of exploration on the dunes

INSIDER TIP

You can arrange with air taxi companies to have bush pilots let you off right on top of the dunes for an easy in-and-out experience. If you have extra time and resources, camping overnight in the Kobuk Valley with a guided outfitter provides a truly immersive experience!

and to the nearby Kobuk River as it meanders through the valley into spruce and alder forests.

Park Snapshot

Your introduction to Kobuk will start in the air as you drink in mesmerizing views of the area before descending to your drop location. Once there, you are smack in one of the most remote (and least visited) national parks with the awaiting adventure of exploring pure wilderness. While you may feel alone, *you are not alone*—this area is filled with life! Half a million caribou migrate through Kobuk twice each year on one of Earth's largest great mammal migrations. This is a prime hunting opportunity for the native Iñupiat, who continue their ancestors' tradition of subsistence living. If you are lucky, you may catch a rare sighting of musk ox, who long ago shared the landscape with woolly mammoths. In the boreal and spruce forests, arctic birds decorate the region with song as a glittering river flows beneath the Ice Age–era mountains of the central Brooks Range.

• WHAT •

Rare arctic sand dunes surrounded by a forested landscape with a river flowing through the area.

• WHERE •

On the eastern perimeter of the park, alongside the Kobuk River.

• WHEN TO VISIT •

May through September during high seasons, after the snow has stopped and when the weather is most predictable. The great caribou migration is best seen by visitors during high season between August and late October, which is also when the sand can be scorching and when thunderstorms are prevalent, which could limit your time on the dunes.

• HOW TO GET THERE •

There are no roads into this remote national park, and only authorized bush plane air taxis are permitted to fly into the park, traveling in from the nearby towns of Kotzebue and Bettles.

Twin Lakes

Your Must-See Guide

Just a quick flight from Lake Clark National Park and Preserve's main access point and visitor center in the small town of Port Alsworth is Twin Lakes—a prime location to jump off into the trailless wilderness of southern Alaska, where backcountry experiences are realized in rivers, lakes, and forests, and on the craggy Neacola Mountains (the southernmost extension of the great Alaska Range).

Upper Twin Lake is six miles long, and its neighbor to the west, Turquoise Lake, is four miles long. Each lake has water so pure that you almost can't imagine being there without getting on the water to paddle or line a fish.

A great place to start your adventure is at Upper Twin Lake, where, upon arriving by a float or bush plane, you can set up camp at established campgrounds or at backcountry locations on or near the lake near Richard Proenneke's Cabin. Proenneke has earned a cult following and is regarded as one of the finest craftsmen ever to live in the Alaskan bush. Starting in 1968 and over the course of three decades, Proenneke applied engineering acumen to construct a homestead complete with a log cabin and off-ground bear-proof storage as well as the tools required to build everything he needed to withstand the challenging environment.

Of the two Twin Lakes, Turquoise Lake is visited less frequently. Here, tundra hugs rocky shorelines with mountains all around. You'll need a bit of backcountry know-how to explore this

LAKE CLARK BEAR VIEWING

Head to the Cook Inlet on the southeast shores of the park for bear-watching opportunities that rival some of the best in Alaska. There, you can wander alongside coastal brown bears on large stretches of beach as they feed on fish and shellfish in the water and onshore.

area, and with that, you will find peace and solitude in a most beautiful setting.

Park Snapshot

With rugged, untapped land in every direction, you will instantly see why Lake Clark is a best-kept secret among the adventure set. Its ultrapure environment serves as a healthy habitat for wildlife, birds, and fish—and a happy one for outdoor lovers who want to set out into an untrammeled landscape to hike great trails by day and find peace under the stars at night.

Lake Clark itself is a forty-mile-long body of water made perfectly blue by sediment that tumbles into it from surrounding glaciers and steel-gray volcanic mountains. Skirting the rocky shores are sprawls of soft tundra, peat mosses, and eco-diverse marshes that are vital to the ecosystem. To the native Dena'ina Athabascan who have lived in the region for more than ten thousand years, the naturally rich environment enables their subsistence way of life to continue uninterrupted. For visitors, the grand size, scale, and undeniable beauty leave them with a longing for more.

• WHAT •

Two large lakes sitting adjacent to one another in a pristine wilderness setting. This area is known as a hub for incredible backcountry adventures and is home to a historic log cabin with a really cool backstory.

• WHERE •

In the central area of the park on the western edge.

• WHEN TO VISIT •

June through October, when weather is warm and services including lodging, transportation, and guided experiences are most widely available.

• HOW TO GET THERE •

Hop in a floatplane and fly from Alaska's capital city of Anchorage. Most scheduled routes fly directly to Port Alsworth, where you can hop on a charter flight to Turquoise Lake, but air taxis can go directly there if you make arrangements ahead of time.

Kennecott Mines and Kennicott Glacier

AK

Your Must-See Guide

In Wrangell-St. Elias, you'll want to make plans to explore both natural and historical points of interest to make the most of your time in America's largest national park. By pairing a visit to the Kennicott Glacier and the Kennecott Mines, you're in for a taste of Alaska's cultural history and a memorable voyage into a treasured backcountry area in Alaska.

The town of Kennecott is the park's most accessible area, where a turn-of-the-century copper mine abandoned in 1938 provides a

MCCARTHY AND NEBESNA ROADS

There are two primitive driving roads into the main area of the park (and few rental agencies allow their fleet to travel them). Nebesna and McCarthy Roads are both rough and irregularly maintained, and neither has fuel or service stops—so head out equipped and prepared and bring a spare (or two!).

glimpse of how the community of McCarthy came to be. In one of the tallest freestanding wood structures in North America—painted red with white trim and beautiful against the icy mountain backdrop—you can wander on guided or self-guided outings into the well-preserved mines that are listed on the National Register of Historic Places. You will see artifacts left behind by miners from a hundred years ago and tools that are still in working condition today.

Adventures on the Kennicott Glacier can be approached several ways. You can go big and tackle a multiday expedition for an intimate experience with the Alaska wilderness as you cross glacier, tundra, and rocky moraine to alpine lakes while trailblazing dense thickets of alder brush where wildlife can be seen along the way. To take it down a notch for an easier (but still moderately challenging) adventure, strap on some crampons and head out on a half-day trip to Root Glacier, the most accessible area of the vast ice sheet, which is just a one-and-a-half-mile hike from the Kennecott Mines.

Park Snapshot

In the largest US national park—and the world's first designated binational UNESCO World Heritage Site—glaciers meet land, flowing pure waters into braided rivers to feed the tundra landscape. This park is one of the least explored, with fewer than three hundred visitors per day—a speck compared to the most famous parks that can count more than one million visitors on certain days. The challenging terrain ensures a wild adventure. It contains nine of the sixteen highest peaks in North America, so it is no surprise that mountaineering and backpacking are huge draws here, and with few established trails, intrepid outdoor enthusiasts can freely head into the backcountry to ice climb on glaciers, hike, paddle, and fish the flowing waterways. If you want to take your adventures to the sky, you can enjoy a bird's-eye vantage point with experienced bush pilots who know the airways above Alaska better than anyone.

• WHAT •

One of Alaska's most visible large glaciers with a historical mining camp from the gold rush era nearby.

• WHERE •

In the central area of the park.

• WHEN TO VISIT •

Wrangell-St. Elias is open from the last Monday of May (Memorial Day in the United States) and the first Monday of September (Labor Day).

• HOW TO GET THERE •

Visitors driving in on McCarthy Road must park their vehicles at the Kennicott River footbridge and travel to the town of McCarthy on foot, by bike, or by taking a privately operated shuttle to McCarthy to link up with guides. The park visitor center is located five miles from McCarthy and sits right by the mines. There are also two-hour charter flights from Anchorage available.

Intermountain Region

The Windows Section

UT

Your Must-See Guide

Starting immediately when you turn off the park road to enter the Windows Section of Arches, you are greeted by a large stone formation called Balanced Rock—think of it as your welcome to the area with one great site already marked off the list. From there, you can either (1) catch a quick view of nearby arches with some success from the parking lot or (2) walk on a well-maintained path into the wind-carved landscape (option 2 is recommended!). A short trail and easy hike lead to

views of North and South Windows (together nicknamed the Spectacles for their resemblance to reading glasses) and Turret Arch, which you can frame perfectly in the center of North Window's opening. A wander to Double Arch brings you to the tallest arch in the park from base to top, and the second-longest free-standing arch (Landscape Arch in a different area of the park is the longest). You can see all of this in the space of just two miles.

On the back side of the arches that face the parking lot is a primitive loop trail that provides an opposite perspective of the sandstone formations. Explore this trail to extend time in the area while checking out ecological interests such as fragile cryptobiotic crust and desert vegetation. At night, this is a great area to enjoy immaculately starry night skies long after the sun falls onto the horizon, without having to hike too far back to your car in the dark.

"TIPTOE ON THE CRYPTO"

Cryptobiotic crust is a thin layer of bioorganic compounds that protect soft earth. These compounds eventually become arches. When trampled, the crust is destroyed, and for this reason, walking off-trail is prohibited apart from designated backcountry paths, slickrock, and washes. Do your part to protect the fragile area—mind the signs.

Park Snapshot

Arches is one of those national parks where you feel the elements of nature at work all around you—sculpting golden earthly formations that seem to sing against the clear blue skies of Utah. It is also an area where there are so many cool places to go and countless incredible things to see and do that building your itinerary is both fun and challenging unless you have an endless amount of time to spend there.

There are more than two thousand arch formations within the park's boundaries and thousands of naturally formed oddities including spires, balanced rocks, pinnacles, and gargoyles found along hiking trails that will make you want to wander on forever.

Part of the draw of Arches is the area where it sits—just four miles from the lively desert town of Moab where services and gear are at the ready, and just a short twenty-eight miles to its neighboring national park, Canyonlands.

• WHAT •

One of the most scenic areas in the national park, with a large collection of arches and other cool rock formations.

• WHERE •

In the central-east area of the park.

• WHEN TO VISIT •

This area of Arches is open year-round. April, May, September, and October are considered the best times to visit, when the weather is mild. Shoulder seasons can turn up dramatic skies that provide an interesting backdrop to some of the most photogenic arches in the park.

• HOW TO GET THERE •

From the visitor center at the entrance of the park, drive about nine miles along Arches Entrance Road and turn right immediately after Balanced Rock. Drive two and a half miles to the parking area, from where you can wander into the Windows Section.

Delicate Arch

UT

Your Must-See Guide

Delicate Arch is a beloved icon of the state of Utah, emblazoned on commemorative state quarters and on the Utah license plate. It is the largest freestanding arch in the park with a forty-six-foot-high and thirty-two-foot-wide opening at its center. Striated colors band throughout the ornately chiseled formation that perches on the top of the hillside overlooking wide valleys where you can see the snowcapped La Sal mountain range in the distance.

HEAT ADVISORY

During the summer months, it can be extremely hot around Delicate Arch (and in Arches in general), with temperatures often creeping over 100°F. There is also little to no shade on the main trail to Delicate Arch, and the sandstone rocks absorb the heat, making the area feel even hotter. If you are traveling to Delicate Arch in the summer, try to avoid midday hikes and opt for visiting around sunset or sunrise.

While you can catch a faraway glimpse of Delicate Arch from the main park road, standing inside its window is the only way to experience the arch for many—especially at sunrise and sunset when it blazes bright orange while kissed by the sun. The path to its doorstep is a three-mile out-and-back hike on the Delicate Arch Trail that climbs and descends a steep four hundred and eighty feet to views that are worth every sweaty step. If taking this route, be sure to stop at the Wolfe Ranch cabin at the trailhead and check out the well-preserved Ute Indian petroglyphs that emblazon the wall there.

Another way to see Delicate Arch is from one mile away from the Lower Delicate Arch Viewpoint, positioned about one hundred yards from the parking lot. A third, and favorite, way to view it is the hike to the Upper Delicate Arch Viewpoint—a one-mile out-and-back hike with some steep climbs and route-finding that lead to excellent views from the top that peer across a gorge canyon.

While you can catch a faraway glimpse of Delicate Arch from the main park road, standing inside its window is the only way to experience the arch for many—especially at sunrise and sunset when it blazes bright orange while kissed by the sun.

• WHAT •

One of the most famous geological formations in the world and the official symbol of Utah.

• WHERE •

Approximately twelve miles from the national park entrance and visitor center, off the main park road.

• WHEN TO VISIT •

April, May, September, and October are considered by many to be the best months, when the weather is mild and warm. June through August brings sweltering heat, and thunderstorms can cause flash flooding, which can create dangerous conditions for canyon hiking. Winter at Arches serves up temperate weather; however, snow can create slick surface conditions.

• HOW TO GET THERE •

From the visitor center at the park entrance, drive thirteen miles along Arches Scenic Drive and turn right on Delicate Arch Road. Drive just over one mile to the Wolfe Ranch parking where the trailhead is located.

Santa Elena Canyon

TX

Your Must-See Guide

The natural river border separating the US and Mexico runs sixty-nine miles along the southern boundary of Big Bend, and a journey into the Santa Elena Canyon is one of the most popular ways to explore it.

With dramatic fifteen-hundred-foot limestone canyon walls towering over the Rio Grande, you are in for plenty of beauty along shaded trails and waterways that make for great hiking and paddling. The Santa Elena Canyon Trail is one of the most visited routes in the park for walking, hiking, and

running on a one-and-a-half-mile out-and-back nature trail. After passing through desert scrubland and crossing Terlingua Creek, the trail climbs a series of switchbacks before descending into the canyon and to the river, where huge boulders surround you from every side.

If you are up for a guided river adventure, regional outfitters can help you plan your desired course. Experienced paddlers can head out on their own. There are car-accessible put-in and pullout locations allowing for more time on the river. Overnight and multiday trips start at Lajitas, where a leisurely thirteen-mile course begins downstream through a varying desert ecosystem. The last seven miles bring you into the canyon where you will pass through Class 4 rapids. Day trips paddle upstream from the Santa Elena Canyon Trailhead returning downstream.

However you choose to experience the canyon, whether it be a short hike or spending a few days there, you will leave with memorable experiences in one of the most visited areas in the park.

Park Snapshot

Texas's nickname is the "Lone Star State," but at Big Bend, there are tens of thousands of visible stars on moonless nights in this International Dark Sky Park. The park was named after the natural "Big Bend" in the Rio Grande River, and scenic points of interest stretch far northward of the international border that hugs the southern part of the state. It is one of the largest, most remote, and least visited national parks. After a day there, you'll be enchanted by the beauty of the rugged Chihuahuan Desert. There are boundless adventures to experience in Big Bend, whether it be exploring scenic drives and backcountry roads where roadrunners, jackrabbits, and lizards dart through the landscape; pitching a tent in established and primitive campgrounds; or hiking trails to historical sites and natural landmarks—you will likely find that the long desert days fly by during your time in this park.

• WHAT •

A dramatic scenic canyon cut by the Rio Grande and one of the main attractions in Big Bend.

• WHERE •

On the southwest edge of the national park, on the US and Mexico border.

• WHEN TO VISIT •

September through May provides the best weather for hiking and the best water flow for rafting on overnight or day trips through the canyon. Head out during the morning hours or at the end of the day for hikes, when crowds are fewer and shade cover is cast by the canyon walls.

• HOW TO GET THERE •

Travel from the park's headquarters at Panther Junction along the Ross Maxwell Scenic Drive or from Old Maverick Road to Castolon and continue to the road's end and parking area.

Chisos Mountains

 TX

Your Must-See Guide

The Chisos Mountains are the only mountain range contained entirely inside a US national park and are a must-explore area in Big Bend, bringing you to the highest section of the park (around seventy-five hundred feet) where among rocky peaks, views stretch out onto the weathered landscape of the Chihuahuan Desert. At higher elevations among diverse forests of Douglas fir, aspen, Arizona cypress, maple, and ponderosa pine, there are throngs of birds, butterflies, and wildlife sighting opportunities to be had (this is black bear and mountain lion habitat!).

Access is made easy along Chisos Basin Road, which leads along a circular valley to an established campground, dining, and lodging at the Chisos Mountains Lodge (the only accommodations in the national park; you can relax here with a drink in hand overlooking the landscape) and the Chisos Basin Visitor Center, where you can obtain permits and information.

Along the road are trailheads from which you can set out on day hikes and overnight backpacks into forested woodlands that seem a world away from all you've seen in the lowlands. The Chisos Basin has extensive trail networks that range from short mile-long wanders to round-trip hikes that bring you deeper into the ecosystem on longer excursions, including a monster twenty-two-mile out-and-back trail

CHISOS

There are several theories about how the Chisos Mountains got their name. Some people say that *chisos* means "ghost," and the mountains were named for the Apache chief Alsate, who at one time had to hide in the mountains. Another theory is that *chisos* was a mispronunciation of the Spanish *hechizos*, meaning "bewitchment" or "enchantment." However, it seems most likely that the mountain range was named after the Chisos tribe.

from the base of the mountain—all remarkable ways to explore the Chisos Basin on foot. Regardless of your hiking plans, know that an extensive network of trails is available to you.

At higher elevations among diverse forests of Douglas fir, aspen, Arizona cypress, maple, and ponderosa pine, there are throngs of birds, butterflies, and wildlife sighting opportunities to be had.

• WHAT •

Forested mountains perched atop the Texas high ground with big hiking and bigger views.

• WHERE •

In the central area of the park, spanning twenty miles outward from Punta de la Sierra to Panther Junction.

• WHEN TO VISIT •

October through April is generally considered the best span of time to visit Big Bend. You'll experience pleasant weather then, although December and January can have cold snaps. The temperature in the Chisos Mountains is five to ten degrees cooler during the day than in the lowlands.

• HOW TO GET THERE •

Panther Junction is home to the park headquarters and is an ideal starting point for adventures into the highlands. Head out on Chisos Basin Road to follow the seven-mile (paved but steep) roadway into the scenic mountain area.

South Rim Road

CO

Your Must-See Guide

South Rim Road is without question the easiest way to experience the magnificent (and dizzying) views of the Black Canyon of the Gunnison. Located on the south—and most frequently visited—side of the park, the scenic roadway leads to pullouts that stand directly on the canyon just steps from your car or to short hikes where you can catch your breath as you approach chasm views that fall deep into the dark canyon.

Right away, you will approach two viewpoints along the Oak Flat Trail, a loop trail of just over one mile and a moderate gain. Look for animal tracks along the way because wildlife loves this area as much as park visitors do. Then venture on to more stops where even broader views of the colorful striated walls of quartz monzonite come into focus if you catch the light just right.

The Painted Wall Overlook, composed of gneiss and schist rock, is a favorite, climbing 2,250 feet from river to rim, a relic of the Precambrian age—the oldest era of Earth's formation shaped nearly two billion years ago. From Chasm View, look for technical rock climbers tackling one of the narrowest portions of the canyon.

Only about thirty minutes of daylight penetrate the canyon walls daily, and that time of day varies depending on the time of year, so while you might not see the walls, you are sure to see the blackness that earned the park its name (and part of what makes the viewing experience so intense here).

DRIVE TO THE BOTTOM OF THE CANYON

At the base of the canyon is the Gunnison River, where fly-fishers drop lines into the river on a quest to snag rainbow and brown trout beneath skyward views onto the canyon. The river is accessible by vehicle on East Portal Road and is also a great area for camping.

🛡 Park Snapshot

Black Canyon is a hidden jewel in the park system, and the vertical canyon walls are unforgettable in every way imaginable.

The park is relatively challenging to explore in terms of accessibility. There are only a few established trails, and most of the protected area lies within the canyon enfolding some of the sheerest cliff faces you've ever seen. There are two areas that line the rim on the north and south sides, with no bridge in between. But none of this should be a deterrent—there are many cool ways to enjoy this park!

The South Rim is the most popular area. Here, you will find the visitor center, services, and accessible viewpoints of the dramatic scenery. The North Rim is quieter. There is an established campground where you can pitch a tent in a shaded pinyon and juniper forest before heading off onto North Rim Road where six overlook viewpoints and hiking trails await.

• WHAT •

A fourteen-mile (round-trip) paved scenic roadway leading to some of the best viewpoints in the most visited area of the national park.

• WHERE •

In the south section of the park, stretching seven miles between Tomichi Point to High Point.

• WHEN TO VISIT •

The weather is best from April through October. South Rim Road is closed to vehicles beyond the visitor center for the remainder of the year. July has the highest number of visitors.

• HOW TO GET THERE •

After passing the entrance sign that welcomes you to Black Canyon of the Gunnison National Park, drive to the entrance station and pay an entry fee, then travel just over one mile farther to Tomichi Point, where you begin the South Rim Road scenic drive.

Sunset Point

UT

Your Must-See Guide

Sunset Point is usually on everyone's must-see list while in Bryce Canyon because it offers a wide-angle, panoramic view of a red rock forest of towering hoodoo formations and tightly condensed networks of fins that sprawl onto the horizon. The canyon is sometimes referred to as the "Silent City" (it was said by settler and park namesake Ebenezer Bryce to be "a hell of a place to lose a cow"). Sunset Point is also, as the name implies, one of the best places in the park to catch the sunset when the canyon is drenched in golden light.

CHECK THE WEATHER

Bryce Canyon resides more than one mile above sea level, bringing cooler temperatures and more extreme weather changes occurring throughout the year. Check weather conditions with the rangers at the visitor center, bring plenty of water and a rain jacket, and layer up.

The viewpoint looks out onto a vast sea of deposits of the ancient Claron formation, which was formed of rivers and lakes millions of years ago and provides a snapshot of Earth's history in its limestone rock and dense mineral compounds. Such wonder gave rise to some of the most iconic formations in the landscape, such as Thor's Hammer, a balanced rock standing on its own just beneath the overlook.

Another cool thing about this spot isn't seen in what's anchored before you but in the sky above, as birds swoop in to perch on branches of old-growth Douglas fir trees—you'll see swallows, Steller's jays, hawks, Clark's nutcrackers, and ravens all catching air in the high-elevation winds that circulate throughout the canyon. If you are up for a hike, wander the Rim Trail from Sunset Point to Sunrise Point, where along the one-mile flat walkway you can enjoy magnificent views of the amphitheater.

Park Snapshot

There is much to explore at Bryce Canyon, but there is no area more enthralling than the Bryce Amphitheater—where you can witness the largest collection of hoodoos on Earth. Bryce Canyon is not technically a canyon, though there are plenty of down-facing lookout points that make it seem like it is. It's actually a six-square-mile labyrinth of naturally painted rocks that have been carved over millions of years.

The high-elevation environment sitting above eight thousand feet allows the continuous carving and shaping of the formations with its thin air, hot and cold temperatures, and strong blustery winds that allow the natural landscape to flourish in its unique way.

The areas of the park that are less lauded but equally worthy of exploring lie on the west side of the park and in perimeter areas just outside of the park on the Paunsaugunt Plateau, where you can experience a more remote meeting with the area.

• WHAT •

A lookout viewpoint that peers onto some of Bryce Canyon's most dramatic and well-known hoodoo formations with surrounding forest and birdlife that frequents the area.

• WHERE •

Between Sunset Point and Inspiration Point a mile from the main park visitor center on the east side of the national park.

• WHEN TO VISIT •

Year-round from dawn until dusk. May through September is the busiest time of year, with the most ranger-led activities and the warmest weather. Sunrise and sunset are popular times at this viewpoint.

• HOW TO GET THERE •

From the park entrance, drive south and follow the signage for Sunrise Point to the parking area and walk about five hundred feet to the viewing platform.

Navajo Loop and Queen's Garden Trail

UT

Your Must-See Guide

If viewing Bryce Canyon Amphitheater from viewpoint on the rim makes you feel as though you're looking upon another planet, then wandering into its landscape will make you feel like you are exploring one!

The Navajo Loop and Queen's Garden Trail is one of the most popular pathways into the heart of the largest collection of hoodoos on Earth, where the mazes reveal complex arrangements of land in an entirely different way than they do from overlook viewpoints along the rim. Hoodoos, spires, canyons, and sky-high balanced rocks take on new life when you see them up close while walking at their bases through narrow corridors. The moderately strenuous three-mile loop enters a vast network of iconic inner-canyon wonders such as Thor's Hammer, the Two Bridges, and Queen Victoria formations. On the path, you might spot the occasional Douglas fir enveloped by ancient geology. The intersection at the Queen's Garden is a wonderful place to stop and have a rest and a snack while capturing photographs of the otherworldly environment and taking in all that surrounds you.

If you are eager to branch off onto connecting offshoot trails, there are plenty of intersecting networks leading to lesser-seen areas along inner-canyon routes. Plan on sharing the trail with plenty of hikers and bikers from spring through fall, as this trail is both a popular and wonderful place to be.

A "GARDEN" FIT FOR A QUEEN

The Queen's Garden Trail is considered an easy hike, but it does have some steep inclines. Also, it is one of the most exposed hikes in Bryce Canyon, so be sure to bring plenty of water and a hat. The Queen's Garden hike includes the Queen Victoria hoodoo overlooking her garden. See if you can spot her and use your imagination to surmise what she is standing on.

The intersection at the Queen's Garden is a wonderful place to stop and have a rest and a snack while capturing photographs of the otherworldly environment and taking in all that surrounds you.

• WHAT •

A popular hike leading into Bryce Canyon Amphitheater where you can wander through hoodoo and spire formations along a trail that is just under three miles.

• WHERE •

North and west of the central area of the park, near the main park visitor center and popular amenities on the western edge of Bryce Canyon.

• WHEN TO VISIT •

March through October, when the weather is warmer at high elevations and when trails are free of ice and snow.

• HOW TO GET THERE •

Drive south from the park entrance and follow signage leading to the parking area near Sunrise Point, where the trail begins and ends. There are sign markers that point to the trailhead just a short walk from the parking lot.

Grand View Point

Your Must-See Guide

Winding through the Island in the Sky section of Canyonlands is a twenty-four-mile (round-trip) paved scenic park road that leads to one of the most celebrated sites in the park at Grand View Point, which is considered by many to be one of the best views of them all at Canyonlands. At 6,080 feet, an extensive field of red rock canyon landscape in the Monument Basin stretches out to meet the mountains and a blue-sky horizon. You'll feel like you can see all of wild Utah in the distance, with the Colorado River and the Needles and Maze districts in view.

It is also a great place to explore on foot with several opportunities to branch off onto spur trails, including a two-mile offshoot that leads to a second overlook. Biking is another popular draw to the roadway, whether it be to take a leisurely stroll or a heart-pounding trip to the end of the road. Because the site is so popular, there are many activities organized by the National Park Service, including daily ranger talks and night sky programs that allow you to linger under the stars while learning about visible planets and clusters of the universe.

Whether you have a half day or longer to explore this area, you are in for a fun and engaging experience that offers a variety of perspectives of a canyon landscape that is as sublime as you can imagine, with pull-offs to several jaw-dropping scenic overlooks along the way.

TRAVEL OFF-PEAK MONTHS

The best times to visit Canyonlands weather-wise are the spring and fall, as the temperatures are warm but not blazing hot, and the nights are cool but comfortable. However, because these are the best weather times, they are also the most crowded. If you are looking for a bit more solitude and quiet, try visiting in the winter months. It will be cold (temperatures get below freezing at night and sometimes during the day too), but the park will be practically empty of crowds.

Park Snapshot

Meandering corridors of colorful canyons cut by mighty rivers make Canyonlands as fun to photograph as it is to explore. By day, outdoor adventures and cultural activities welcome you at every turn. At dusk, you'll be treated to views beneath soft desert skies that paint the desert landscape. And if you are a night owl, you can experience the wonder of Utah stargazing in what is one of nine International Dark Sky Parks in the state.

Canyonlands National Park is split into four sections. Island of the Sky is the most visited and accessible area and is great for auto-touring and day hikes. The Needles district has some of the best backpacking trails, campsites, and slot canyons around. The Maze district is the most remote and rugged area of the park and a prime spot for experienced backcountry adventurers. The Colorado and Green Rivers serve up water-based expeditions on self-propelled watercraft.

• WHAT •

An iconic viewpoint with panoramic scenery and easy hiking trails along the mesa.

• WHERE •

The southernmost point of the Island in the Sky section, in the north-central area of the park.

• WHEN TO VISIT •

The trail is open year-round, and all seasons offer a lovely experience in different ways. Spring and fall have the best temperatures. July and August are hot, so bring weather protection. Ice and snow may be present during winter, so bring microspikes and/or shoes with solid tread if heading out during that time, but expect an interesting take on the scenery.

• HOW TO GET THERE •

Drive south from the Island in the Sky Visitor Center along the scenic drive to the main viewpoint where you can catch the view or hike onward.

Chesler Park

Your Must-See Guide

While Island in the Sky is the most visited section in Canyonlands, the Needles district may be the most beloved for those looking to immerse themselves in a more remote and secluded area. If you are a lover of the backcountry, the sweeping scenery and challenging routes are sure to leave you longing for more. You can trot out on day hikes in the area or opt for a multi-day backpacking adventure leading to fanciful valleys before entering slot canyons where you are 100 percent hidden from view.

The best, and only, way to explore Chesler Park is on foot—and the Chesler Park Loop Trail is your conduit into many incredible areas with several options to modify your route. It has a strenuous start as you ascend a small ridge where you can stop and take in unbelievable views of striated formations before turning back. If you are keen to push on, there is a six-mile route on this trail through slickrock to an overlook that peers out onto a colorful desert wonderland.

More immersive experiences can be undertaken on the ten-and-a-half-mile trail that meets the Joint Trail. Along with the unbeatable views, you will traverse rock scrambles, peaceful hiking in Chesler Canyon, and a journey into a slot canyon.

If ten-plus miles in one day sounds overly ambitious, you can break up your adventure by hiking half of the ten-mile loop and camping in the Chesler Park backcountry (with a wilderness permit), where you can enjoy solitude and rest your head beneath the stars.

NAVIGATION TIP

There is considerable route-finding along the trails in the Chesler Park area. Look for cairns (stacked stone piles) that will help guide your way. Take photographs along the way to note landmarks and formations in the background for reference to help guide your way back.

If you are a lover of the backcountry, the sweeping scenery and challenging routes are sure to leave you longing for more. You can trot out on day hikes in the area or opt for a multiday backpacking adventure leading to fanciful valleys before entering slot canyons.

• WHAT •

A large meadow circled by colorful cedar mesa sandstone formations in a secluded area. Chesler Park is considered by many to provide some of the best backcountry hiking in the park.

• WHERE •

In the Needles district, in the southwest area of the national park.

• WHEN TO VISIT •

February through November. The spring and fall time frames are the most prized, as the weather is most temperate compared to the height of summer during the rainy season, when temperatures soar and thunderstorms are common. You can also expect fewer crowds during shoulder seasons, which offers a more intimate experience.

• HOW TO GET THERE •

Start from the Needles Visitor Center and head three miles into the park on a passable dirt road to the Elephant Hill Trailhead in Soda Spring.

Fruita Historic District and Scenic Drive

UT

Your Must-See Guide

The Fruita Rural Historic District is the easiest first stop in Capitol Reef, and with a fascinating human and natural history relished at every turn, it is a must-see area while in the national park.

Stories of a native past are preserved in the village of Fruita, which is empty of human habitation today but was once a thriving communal epicenter for the Fremont Indians a thousand years ago. Hidden in the landscape along the Fremont River canyon are historical finds including the Fremont petroglyphs on large panels of golden sandstone that depict a typical hunter-gatherer existence.

In the seventeenth century, Mormon pioneers came to the region and re-created the utopia that had been built by the Fremonts. Fruit trees were planted along centuries-old irrigation lines, and the orchards have since flourished, providing a popular stop during the summer for families and adventure-seekers to harvest fruits such as apples and peaches that fuel bellies along road-trip adventures and on trail hikes into the wild. Scattered throughout the orchards are several historic human-made structures that will teach you more about homesteading, schooling, and a time of prosperity for settlers in the region.

When you are done at Fruita, venture out along a twenty-mile out-and-back scenic drive among dramatic slickrock with stops at trailheads and viewpoints where canyons, ridges, buttes, and badlands travel on far into the distance.

IF YOU HAVE FOUR-WHEEL DRIVE...

Don't miss the Cathedral Valley! The northern area of the park is a backcountry dreamscape with few visitors due to a challenging-to-get-to area that requires four-wheel drive to pass through a small river. While there, be sure to check out the Temple of the Sun and Glass Mountain.

There are eleven stops detailing unique areas and points of interest along the interpretive roadway.

 Park Snapshot

Capitol Reef is the least visited of Utah's five national parks, which is a blessing for park-goers in search of more one-on-one time with the natural beauty and historic sites that abound there. The park is split into three sections: the Cathedral Valley (north); the Waterpocket Fold (south); and, the most visited, the central Fruita Historic area. Each is filled with its own unique tapestry of must-sees—whether it be colorful earthly formations, rivers that cut through the land, a rich human history, or a favorite of geologists: the Waterpocket Fold, the second-largest monocline in North America described as a "wrinkle" in the earth's crust, resembling a coral reef turned inside out.

A journey into the park will reveal ancient rock art and earthly scenery, with wildlife sightings possible at every turn all in one day. Outdoor enthusiasts find themselves on happy ground here, with wilderness trails leading into a backcountry where solitude is met by boundless beauty.

• WHAT •

A rural historic district that preserves native and settler history of the area, is home to the main park visitor center, and serves as the gateway to a scenic drive through a curious geological wonderland.

• WHERE •

In the southern section of the park, seven miles from the west entrance and eight and a half miles from the east entrance.

• WHEN TO VISIT •

Mid-June through October, when the orchards are open to visitors for harvesting fruit. If you visit during off-season, you will experience fewer crowds, which can make the area feel like the ghost town it used to be when it was abandoned nearly a hundred years ago.

• HOW TO GET THERE •

From either entrance, travel into the park on the primary access point on UT-24 (one of two paved roads existing in the national park).

Cathedral Valley

UT

Your Must-See Guide

Cathedral Valley is where solitude, spectacular scenery, and backcountry bliss converge in a wild and remote wilderness ecosystem. This area is infrequently visited because it is a bit of an effort both to get to and to explore there—and that's part of its allure.

The self-guided, fifty-eight-mile Cathedral Valley Driving Loop tour will bump you along the rocky roadway surrounded by bands of colorful bentonite hills that striate the landscape in rainbow hues. In Upper and Lower Cathedral Valley, towering sculpted entrada sandstone monoliths are among the area's most captivating features, including the Walls of Jericho and Temple of the Sun, Temple of the Moon, and Temple of the Stars, which are especially beautiful places to catch the sunrise or sunset if overnighting in the primitive campgrounds. Other cool points of interest include Glass Mountain, Gypsum Sinkhole, and historic Morrell Cabin.

Experiencing such wonder requires some preparation. Check for road closures in advance to learn if there are impassable areas. The Fremont River (which you'll need to cross) has no bridge and may experience flooding. Snow and rain in winter, spring, and summer can wash out roads, making travel impossible for even the most souped-up vehicles. Prepare for the unexpected and head in well equipped. Emergency service may be hours or days away, and there

GLASS MOUNTAIN

Glass Mountain is not actually made of glass but rather is an exposed mound of selenite crystals. The crystals in this mountain are unusual both in size and quantity. While they are beautiful to behold, remember that it is illegal to collect any rock, plant, or animal from a national park, so admire the crystals, but don't gather them.

is rarely cell reception. Bring emergency supplies, a spare tire, shovel, food, and water (there is no potable water in this area of the park). Ask anyone who has explored there, and they'll assure you that it is well worth the effort.

In Upper and Lower Cathedral Valley, towering sculpted entrada sandstone monoliths are among the area's most captivating features.

• WHAT •

A remote and rugged area with fascinating geology, eroded sandstone formations, and vast panoramic views.

• WHERE •

On the northwestern edge of the national park, in the North (Cathedral Valley) District.

• WHEN TO VISIT •

April, May, September, and October have the best weather at Capitol Reef. Summer temperatures soar, and winter temperatures plunge, making travel in the backcountry more of a challenge.

• HOW TO GET THERE •

Most visitors come from the Fruita Historic District fifty-eight miles south, traveling the eastern edge of the park boundary along Hartnett Road. You'll need a high-clearance vehicle to make a small river crossing before entering the area. There are two other entrance points—northeast via Cathedral Road, and Polk Creek Road on the northwest side.

NM

The Big Room

Your Must-See Guide

The Big Room is a grand underground gallery of living artwork! Evolving over millions of years, the caverns are known for their ornate decorations and fantastical formations including tubes, spires, ribbons, drapes, and curtains. From the dank grounds, columns stand sturdy like trees, and stalagmites rise from the cave floor like root systems; from the ceilings, stalactites drip like light fixtures. You will see large named formations such as the Rock of Ages, the Giant Dome, the Painted Grotto, and a rope

LEARN WHILE EXPLORING

Pick up an audio tour guide from the visitor center to learn about the cave's geological and exploratory history, and more about the formations found there. The narration could range from scientific concepts such as how acidic groundwater morphed the caves to stories of explorers from long ago.

ladder falling into a gaping hole that remains from a 1924 expedition.

Floor space in the Big Room covers an area of at least eight acres, and having a little bit of extra space around you can open your eyes to the mysterious world in remarkable ways (and stave off feelings of claustrophobia for those adverse to confined spaces). The trail is one and a quarter miles on even, well-lit ground, and the lighting is helpful for capturing photographs without the need for extensive camera gear and tripods, which aren't permitted.

The Park Service has made a visit to the Big Room as easy as possible, with an elevator descending directly from the visitor center enabling anyone to explore the area, even in a short amount of time. If you have the inclination and ability to hike it, the Natural Entrance Trail allows for a longer experience. It descends seven hundred and fifty feet into a grand showroom where large formations set the tone of what a cave looks like and what being underground feels like before entering the sophisticated Big Room.

 Park Snapshot

Hidden beneath the surface of the Guadalupe Mountains is a limestone-carved wonderworld with one hundred and nineteen mapped caves adorned by strange formations that have evolved over the course of two hundred and sixty-five million years. The longer you look, the more you will uncover—spurring imagination as you ponder ideas such as initial discovery, rediscovery, and how the mysterious subterranean environment was formed in the first place and became what it is today.

One of the most unique experiences in the park occurs during the annual bat flight. Every year from late May through October, hundreds of thousands of Brazilian free-tailed bats fly from their home underground through the Natural Cave Entrance and into the sky at dusk. As they flitter above the landscape, you are surrounded by a desert-studded paradise with rocky canyons, ancient sea ledges, flowering cactus, and desert-adapted animals and birds that have found a way to thrive in the arid Chihuahuan Desert.

• WHAT •

A self-guided tour of the largest underground natural limestone cave chamber in the Western Hemisphere.

• WHERE •

On the northeast edge of the park, underground.

• WHEN TO VISIT •

The Big Room is open year-round with cavern temperatures a consistent 56°F. Visiting during May through October will ensure the most available tours into the cave and the best weather for aboveground hiking (though it is hot from June through August). It is also when you can experience the Park Service's Bat Flight Program.

• HOW TO GET THERE •

Head to the Carlsbad Caverns National Park Visitor Center where you can buy tickets, then descend an elevator located in the visitor center directly to the Big Room. You can also choose to extend your adventure with the Natural Entrance Trail hike that adjoins the Big Room.

MT

Going-to-the-Sun Road

Your Must-See Guide

With the unveiling of Going-to-the-Sun Road in 1933, Governor Frank H. Cooney said, "There is no highway which will give the seer, the lover of grandeur of the Creator's handiwork, more thrills, more genuine satisfaction deep in his being, than will a trip over this road." Today, it is among Glacier's main attractions and one of the most iconic scenic driving roads in North America.

The fifty-mile highway cuts through a one-million-acre wilderness of evergreen forests that kiss the snowcapped peaks decorating the horizon of Big Sky, Montana. At

KNOW BEFORE YOU GO

There is no fuel in the national park, there are vehicle size and height restrictions on Going-to-the-Sun Road, and reservations are now required to travel the road. Be sure to gas up and look for the latest info at the official park website, www.nps.gov/glac, for info before you head in.

Logan Pass (6,646 feet), you will find yourself engulfed by raw scenery when you hit the Continental Divide, an ecological feature separating watersheds that feed into the Pacific and Atlantic Oceans. At this high elevation, alpine wildflowers spread across the landscape during July, and you are likely to spot wildlife such as mountain goats and bighorn sheep that are consistently seen there all peak season. Elk, moose, and birdlife are commonly seen as well.

The Logan Pass Visitor Center provides a great stopping point for services and to gather information about the best hikes in the area. A popular and beautiful hike starting at the visitor center is along the Hidden Lake Trail to the Hidden Lake Overlook, with views of Bearhat Mountain peering overhead. Six and a half miles from the park entrance, stop for a picturesque view and photo opportunity of Wild Goose Island on Saint Mary Lake with dramatic mountain peaks reflecting in the glacial waters.

Park Snapshot

Glacier is a favorite among national park-goers, with endless adventures to be realized and boundless beauty to encounter along the way. Ironically, glaciers are scarcer than ever in the national park as a result of warmer winters bringing more rain and less snow from which glaciers are formed; meanwhile, glaciers are what created everything you are witness to while there, all carved over time by the dynamic forces of the Rocky Mountains. Within the peaks are glacier lakes, conifer forests, sloped meadows, fertile valleys, and pure waterways—all of which provide healthy habitats for animals, fish, and birdlife.

All summer, the park becomes a haven for camping and fishing adventures, road-tripping, and photography opportunities. Day hikes, long-distance treks, leisurely nature walks, and hardcore backpacking adventures are made easier with a vast network along seven hundred miles of established paths. During winter, Glacier is a premier destination for mountaineering, cross-country skiing, and snowshoeing. In autumn, the landscape explodes with golden fall foliage that peeks out from an evergreen wilderness.

• WHAT •

A historic transmountain highway cutting through rugged, mountainous national parkland.

• WHERE •

Running west-east through the central area of the park.

• WHEN TO VISIT •

July through mid-October is the best window of time to travel the full length of Going-to-the-Sun Road, but access can be limited on occasion due to weather and snowfall. Lower elevation areas of the road are open year-round.

• HOW TO GET THERE •

In your private vehicle, start at either the east or west entrance and follow fifty miles along Going-to-the-Sun Road with Logan Pass bringing you to the highest point. There is a free shuttle (first come, first served) offered by the Park Service with stops between the Apgar and St. Mary Visitor Centers. There are a couple of private companies offering guided tours as well.

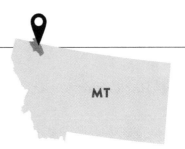

MT

Many Glacier

Your Must-See Guide

While most visits to Glacier focus on accessible points along Going-to-the-Sun Road, exploring the Many Glacier area is a worthwhile way to get off the main road and experience what many believe to be the heart of the park. This is where you will find many of the most popular trails with varying levels of difficulty, including the famed Grinnell

SWIFTCURRENT LAKE

Swiftcurrent Lake is a glacier-fed lake in Glacier National Park surrounded by towering snowcapped peaks. Unlike many of the other lakes in Glacier National Park, Swiftcurrent Lake sees a lot of use. Because the water is cool year-round (often too cold for swimming), this lake is used mostly for recreational purposes such as kayaking and boating. The area is windy, but not as windy as other parts of the park, and fishing is permitted, allowing anglers to try their hand at catching some of the brook trout in its waters.

Glacier, Grinnell Lake, Swiftcurrent Pass, and Iceberg Lake Trails—some of which put on full display the sky-high and jeweled characteristics that earned the park its nickname: "Crown of the Continent."

When you are not pressing your feet against earthen paths, put them to the historic floors of the Many Glacier Hotel and surrounding buildings, a National Historic Landmark that is over one hundred years old. From its deck, you can gaze at Swiftcurrent Lake, look for wildlife with binoculars, and enjoy the peaceful natural setting with a refreshment in hand while recanting sightings from your time there. There are plenty of amenities provided by the hotel, too, including dining, evening ranger programs, and boat cruises leaving from the shore.

On the west side of the lake, there is an iconic view (photo opportunity!) of Grinnell Point rising from the eastern rocky shores that are revealed in the glassy waters. You can stay at the Many Glacier Hotel, though a reservation will need to be booked some time in advance at this popular location. There are also reservable campgrounds and cabins in the area.

On the west side of the lake, there is an iconic view of Grinnell Point rising from the eastern rocky shores that are revealed in the glassy waters.

AZ

Hermit Road

Your Must-See Guide

Hermit Road is the most popular scenic roadway in the Grand Canyon, packing a lot of punch with a large number of stops in one concentrated area. There are nine overlook viewpoints in a span of just seven miles for plenty of opportunities to peer at the geological wonders of the Grand Canyon while learning some of the area history along the way.

The hop-on hop-off approach of shuttle rides allows you to explore for any duration of time—whether that be catching a quick view and moving on or exploring trails on foot

from one viewpoint to the next. This section of paved road is beloved by bicyclists and road runners who want to break a sweat with unparalleled beauty by their side.

One of the first stops is at the Trailview Overlook, looking down upon hairpin switchbacks on the Bright Angel Trail, which leads to the bottom of the canyon, bisecting the forested flanks that carve the valley. Powell Point offers a dose of cultural history where a memorial honors expedition crews that traversed the Colorado River over a century ago. Hopi Point and Mohave Point are known as two of the premier overlooks in the park to catch the sunrise and sunset, opening to wide canyon vistas and glimpses of the Colorado River that has cut the canyon over the course of millions of years. At Pima Point, the first (or last) stop from Hermits Rest, you can on occasion hear a whisper of the Colorado River that roars four thousand feet below.

BOOK IN ADVANCE!

Whether it be a historic lodge stay on the rim, at the bottom of the canyon at Phantom Ranch or Bright Angel Campground, or on a canyon descent by mule—many coveted Grand Canyon experiences require a reservation and are often booked more than a year in advance.

Park Snapshot

Seeing the Grand Canyon in person brings it to life in a way no picture or painting ever could—and the views are just the beginning of all there is to marvel over in this top-visited national park. You can auto-tour or bike along scenic drives, hike the inner canyon and rim in a myriad of ways, capture photographs of marmalade skies at sunset, and take advantage of ranger-led programs and guided trips to learn about the history of the beautiful natural world and the native Havasupai, Hopi, Hualapai, and Navajo who have called it home for more than ten thousand years. Another way to get a taste of this spectacular gash in the earth is on a flightseeing tour to soar above the canyon.

Iconic lodges, amenities, historical sites, exhibits, and other conveniences for visitors are available in most areas of the South Rim just steps from the edge of the canyon.

• WHAT •

A scenic roadway with some of the most celebrated viewpoints in the national park.

• WHERE •

On the South Rim, between Grand Canyon Village, Hermits Rest, and the Hermit Trailhead.

• WHEN TO VISIT •

Hermit Road is open year-round. The park offers a free shuttle bus between dawn and dusk hours with designated stops from March to November. The scenic road is open to private vehicles from December through February.

• HOW TO GET THERE •

Head to the Village Route Transfer station on the west side of Grand Canyon Village and hop on the "red route" shuttle line for a minimum eighty-minute round-trip ride (without stops, so you can plan for at least a half day if not a full day once setting out).

AZ

Bottom of the Canyon

Your Must-See Guide

Spending time inside the Grand Canyon's steep walls and at its base is memorable and rewarding and provides a profoundly different perspective than what you experience on the canyon rim. The farther you descend, the lusher and more verdant it becomes. Your body works a little bit harder, and you begin to understand how tiny you are in comparison to the grandest of canyons—something to ponder and reflect on along your journey.

A TOWN AT THE BOTTOM

Supai Village is located at the base of Havasu Canyon outside of the national park boundary in the Havasupai Indian Reservation. The village has a population of two hundred and eight, and because it is inaccessible by road, it is considered the most remote community in the lower forty-eight states (where mail is still delivered by pack mule). The area is known for its flowing waterfalls and cultural heritage.

Regardless of how you find your way to the bottom, it is not an adventure for the faint of heart, as the base lies four thousand feet from the rim. Guided mule rides can lighten the load and are a historical tradition, transporting passengers into the canyon since the late 1800s.

Classic rim-to-rim hikes start on the North or South Rims and lead to the bottom of the canyon and the Colorado River, then up to the rim on the other side. There are modified rim-to-rim hikes as well—one of the most popular routes being an out-and-back hike descending from the South Rim for seven miles on the South Kaibab Trail and returning ten miles up the Bright Angel Trail. Some choose to do this hike in one day, but it is not recommended—once you set out, you are fully invested and there is no elevator back to the top!

At the bottom, you can pitch a tent at Bright Angel Campground or stay at Phantom Ranch, where hot showers, nightly dinners, and conversations flow freely.

The farther you descend, the lusher and more verdant it becomes. Your body works a little bit harder, and you begin to understand how tiny you are in comparison to the grandest of canyons—something to ponder and reflect on along your journey.

An intimate experience within the inner canyon landscape.

Inside the canyon walls and at the bottom of the Grand Canyon where the Colorado River runs.

April through June, September, and October have cooler but still pleasant temperatures compared to the hotter midsummer months, and the trails remain snow- and ice-free at this time as well.

There are three ways to get to the bottom of the Grand Canyon—on foot on established hiking trails from both the North and South Rims, on a mule ride from the top of the canyon's South Rim, or by raft along the Colorado River (requiring a guided outfitter due to the technical nature of the passage).

Mormon Row Historic District

WY

Your Must-See Guide

Do you want a taste of pioneer history with your national park adventure? Are you determined to capture an iconic photograph symbolic of Grand Teton National Park? Look no further than Mormon Row, where you can head out on a self-guided walking tour in an area that is quintessentially old-time American West. There are twenty-seven homesteads in two separate areas, built over

A TRAIL FOR EVERYONE

The rocks that form the three prominent peaks were carved by ancient glaciers that are among the oldest on Earth, yet the range is one of the youngest in the Rocky Mountain chain. It is an ideal environment to hit trails big and small. Multiday trekking and backpacking adventures can lead to elevations of nearly four thousand feet—and with more than two hundred and thirty miles of maintained trails, visitors of all skill levels can take on the Tetons at their own pace.

the course of decades by Mormon settlers starting in the 1890s. Stretching across the backdrop are the jagged peaks of the snowcapped Teton Range above the Jackson Hole Valley.

The two most well-known and commonly photographed structures are known as the "Moulton Barns" sitting in adjacent areas about a mile off the highway. They were built by brothers John and Thomas Alma (T.A.) Moulton. The John Moulton Barn sits aside a pink stucco house built to replace John Moulton's original log home. The T.A. Moulton Barn is one of the most photographed buildings in the United States, with a roof that is positioned against the Grand Tetons if you catch the angle just right. Another notable stop on Mormon Row is at the Andy Chambers Homestead, which is the most complex of those that remain.

At sunrise, photographers from all over the world form a line to capture the scene in the early morning light when the wood buildings, mountains, and sprawling valley floor are aglow in jeweled colors. Dawn and dusk hours provide the best times of day to see wildlife in the area, such as elk and antelope.

Park Snapshot

With snowcapped mountain peaks almost year-round and a pastoral valley sprawled out beneath it, Grand Teton National Park has earned a spot on the world's most beautiful places list. This is one of those all-interest parks where everyone has something to do, whether it be hiking, camping, paddling, cycling, rock climbing, fishing, or wildlife viewing along scenic drives. The park is a huge draw for photographers, especially when the leaves change color during fall.

• WHAT •

A swath of parkland preserving historic homesteads built in the late 1800s, with stunning views of the Teton Range and Jackson Hole in the background.

• WHERE •

The Gros Ventre/Antelope Flats area in the southeast section of the park, between the towns of Kelly and Moose.

• WHEN TO VISIT •

May through October. Late summer and autumn are especially nice, with great weather, colorful fall foliage, and active wildlife.

• HOW TO GET THERE •

Driving north from the town of Jackson, turn off Highway 191 north of Moose Junction onto Antelope Flats Road and drive about one mile before reaching a small dirt parking area. From there, set out on foot to explore the two sections located north and south of Antelope Flats Road.

Jenny Lake Loop

WY

Your Must-See Guide

No trip to the Tetons could be complete without spending time at Jenny Lake, the most well-known spot in the park and a great place to enjoy a variety of experiences in the most peaceful of natural settings. There are adventures for every kind of visitor, whether it be paddling on self-propelled watercraft (canoe, kayak, stand-up paddleboard), fishing the serene waters, jumping off onto backpacking and climbing excursions in the park, or hitting easier day hikes to waterfalls and awesome viewpoints.

BRING YOUR CAMERA

This is a world-class destination for photographers, featuring some of the most classic national park scenes. Views of the jagged peaks of the Teton Range, wildlife, and seasonal aspects such as wildflowers and fall foliage provide plenty of variety for great photo opportunities the whole of your time there.

The Jenny Lake Loop trail circumnavigates the lake along just over six and a half miles of even pathway with seven hundred feet of elevation gain and offshoots to other great hiking areas—such as popular sites like Hidden Falls and Inspiration Point. Seven and a half miles up from the trailhead, you can catch views of Cascade Canyon and Mount Moran.

Back at the lake, nearly two square miles of pristine mountain water awaits, and because this is one of only two lakes in the park where motorized vehicles are authorized to operate, it is a go-to in the Tetons for watersport play. Jenny Lake Boating provides a shuttle service that runs frequently during high season, making transport to the popular Cascade Canyon trailhead on the west side of the lake easier (shaving four miles there and back).

On the Jenny Lake Scenic Drive, a one-way paved road flanking the eastern edge of the lake, you can catch impressive views of the Tetons from the Jenny Lake Overlook.

There are adventures for every kind of visitor, whether it be paddling on self-propelled watercraft, fishing the serene waters, jumping off onto backpacking and climbing excursions in the park, or hitting easier day hikes to waterfalls and awesome viewpoints.

• WHAT •

A glacier-made lake and focal point in the national park, leading to climbing and hiking routes and with lake access for watersport and transit to other areas of the lake perimeter, where you can head out into different areas.

• WHERE •

Near Moose, Wyoming, just off of Teton Park Road.

• WHEN TO VISIT •

May through October, when hiking trails and lake access are open and when the most services are available.

• HOW TO GET THERE •

From Moose in the south or Jackson Lake Junction in the north, drive on Teton Park Road into the center of the park and turn at South Jenny Lake. Parking is limited—be sure to use the shoulder if parking on Teton Park Road.

Great Sand Dunes

CO

Your Must-See Guide

There are fantastic dunes at several national parks in the United States, but few compare in magnitude to those at Great Sand Dunes—home to Star Dune, the highest in North America, standing at seven hundred and fifty feet. And the fun doesn't stop there! With a thirty-cubic-mile sandbox to play in, visitors of all ages are childlike while gliding down soft slopes on sandboards with belly laughs in tow (head to the park visitor center to obtain information about renting boards).

EXPLORE THE BACKCOUNTRY BY CAR

The Medano Pass Primitive Road provides passage beyond the dunes, entering through a canyon and into the Sangre de Cristo Mountains, where you can explore trails on foot, spot wildlife, and fish for trout in crystal alpine lakes. A four-by-four vehicle is essential to making the journey.

This natural playground caters to those looking for more challenging outdoor sport as well, beckoning endurance hikers and runners to tackle steep slopes at high altitudes. Backpackers disappear into sanctioned areas for camping, the requirement being that they are out of view from the main dunes parking lot. Overnight adventures on the dunes allow visitors to experience what is one of the quietest national parks in the system, and one with very little light pollution, making it one of the best spots for stargazing in the lower forty-eight states. At night, when the crowds are gone and you are alone with your gear and the quiet landscape, it is incredible to find that you are completely absent from human activity apart from your own—and just a four-hour drive from Denver.

Even traveling a short distance onto the dunes changes your perspective as the winds blow patterns beneath your feet. Where the sand remains untouched, you will likely find photographers seeking unique ways to capture the golden hues and subtle textures of Colorado's ancient sands.

Park Snapshot

Great Sand Dunes National Park and Preserve is one of Colorado's best-kept secrets—where you can climb the highest dune field in North America and set off into a mountainous landscape that leads to alpine wilderness all in one day. The park's landscape starts in the San Juan Valley flatland and moves to lowlands marked by Medano Creek, where park-goers play in the waters during spring and summer snowmelt. The dune fields are the star of the park, formed thirty-five million years ago after a volcanic eruption and remaining protected today by the Sangre de Cristo and San Juan Mountains. Tucked into that range are forested foothills that eventually turn to alpine wilderness and tundra at high elevations maxing out at 13,604 feet—so while the dunes are the biggest draw to the area, know that backcountry campers, climbers, and mountaineers are sharing the park with you at any given time.

• WHAT •

Vast sand dunes centered between gorgeous alpine mountains and aquatic lowlands.

• WHERE •

On the southeast edge of the national park near the only park visitor center.

• WHEN TO VISIT •

May typically kicks off the annual flow of Medano Creek, bringing water into the lowlands. Temperatures at this time are warm but not scorching, and afternoon winds soften the air. The months of June through August bring prairie wildflowers that color the landscape, though sands get quite hot during July. September is known to have favorable temperatures and calmer conditions.

• HOW TO GET THERE •

The Great Sand Dunes Parking lot is situated right next to the park visitor center and the Piñon Flats campground. Head to the visitor center first to get information to help you plan your time there.

Guadalupe Peak Texas Highpoint Trail

TX

Your Must-See Guide

Are you a highpointer looking to scratch a new top-of-the-state peak off your list? Or a casual day hiker wanting to explore a diverse ecosystem while scouting for birds, interesting vegetation, and desert wildlife? If any of this sounds great to you, this trail has you covered.

The out-and-back Guadalupe Peak Texas Highpoint Trail travels just over eight miles to its apex towering above the Texas skyline at just under three thousand feet, looking

DOUBLE YOUR NATIONAL PARK EXPERIENCE!

Make the most of your time in this remote region by hitting two national parks in one trip. Pair your adventure to Guadalupe Mountains with a trip to Carlsbad Caverns, which is twenty-five miles away. You can explore the mountains aboveground before traveling underground into decorated caves beneath the New Mexico and Texas state line.

out onto the Chihuahuan Desert. If you zoom in on the area below, you can see the Salt Basin Dunes and maybe even spot your car at the parking area—a reminder of how high you've climbed. Beneath the summit, there are primitive camping sites where you can pitch a tent (if you are up for toting your gear up the mountain).

The great thing about longer, challenging trails like this one is that you can hike its entirety or just part of it, depending on the type of experience you want to have. The first mile and a half is steep along zigzagging switchbacks, but it soon levels out into a small forested area of pinyon pine and Douglas fir trees where bird-watching is at its best. From there, you can head back down to the trailhead for a shorter, modified hike or continue up to where you will want to sign the trail summit registrar to commemorate your journey to the rooftop of Texas. Whatever your speed, this hike reveals some of the coolest aspects of the park from a variety of vantage points.

 Park Snapshot

The high peaks of the Guadalupe mountain range rise more than three thousand feet from the floor of the Chihuahuan Desert to form grand limestone peaks like El Capitan, the area's most prominent peak, and, near it, the Guadalupe Peak standing 8,751 feet above sea level. Within the range is the Capitan Reef—an ancient reef system once buried by a sea, starting in the north side of the park and extending into New Mexico.

There are more than eighty miles of established foot trails where hikers and casual day-trippers can explore wooded areas, thriving grasslands, bright white sand dunes, canyons, and high mountains in one of America's least visited national parks. Don't miss the Frijole Ranch, a small museum that tells the story of Native American communities from the area.

• WHAT •

A hiking trail leading through mixed terrain to the highest peak in Texas.

• WHERE •

On the southeast side of the national park, heading west from the eastern park boundary.

• WHEN TO VISIT •

The trail is open year-round and is beautiful to visit anytime depending on what kind of weather you prefer. Like most of the desert Southwest, summer temperatures can soar but will cool slightly the higher up the mountain you go. Layer up, and plan for unexpected weather changes.

• HOW TO GET THERE •

Start at the Pine Springs Visitor Center, the park's main visitor center and headquarters, and drive one mile to the Pine Springs Trailhead—park, gear up, and travel along the well-marked signage.

Cliff Palace

CO

Your Must-See Guide

Mesa Verde is home to the largest and best-preserved collection of Ancestral Puebloan cliff dwellings in North America, and Cliff Palace is the most sophisticated of them all.

The first stone was stacked around 1200 C.E., and over the course of twenty years, the dwelling would expand to include one hundred and fifty rooms and twenty-three kivas (sacred multipurpose and ceremonial rooms dug into the ground), where an estimated one hundred people lived at the height of its use until it was abandoned one hundred years later. With most dwellings in the park composed of only a few rooms, the size and complexity of Cliff Palace indicate that it held ceremonial and social significance to inhabitants and to surrounding communities.

Your first glimpse will likely be from the Cliff Palace Overlook, where you would be dared not to contemplate how people entered and exited the dwelling, dealt with natural elements, and sourced food and water—all the while pondering what life was generally like there. What did they wear to stay warm? What words and expressions did they use? These questions and others will brim as you journey into your own imagination with your mind's eye on a distant past carefully preserved in southwest Colorado.

Stepping inside Cliff Palace will make you feel large as you duck beneath low doorways and wander corridors upon uneven stone into rooms of various shapes and sizes— some once colorfully painted and

RESPECT THE RESEARCH SITE

Along with the wealth of ancient sites already rediscovered and preserved within the park, there are many more to be found, which makes it an active hub for research and a highly restricted area aimed at cultural preservation. Walking off established trails is entirely prohibited and is strictly enforced.

likely shared by multiple people, and others tiny and difficult to access that likely stored maize, gourds, and grains. The kivas are believed to be where ceremonial rituals took place.

🛡 Park Snapshot

Nearly one thousand years ago, Mesa Verde (Spanish for "green table") was an epicenter of the Ancestral Puebloan people who built their homes on cliffsides and atop the mesa that caps the Navajo Canyon; nestled around them are juniper and pinyon pine forests that blanket the region. Today, the park protects the cultural heritage of twenty-six indigenous tribes and is an active archaeological site where researchers are still uncovering artifacts dating to 550–1300 B.C.E. There are nearly six hundred cliff dwellings and five thousand archaeological sites. Some are small one-room pueblos and pit houses atop the mesa; others are multi-story palaces nestled on cliff ledges between the mesa and the Montezuma Valley floor. The architectural complexity is noteworthy, built with Navajo sandstone, wooden beams, and mortar—a mixture of soil, water, ash, and rocks used to fill gaps while strengthening construction.

• WHAT •

The largest of the six hundred Ancestral Puebloan cliff dwellings in Mesa Verde.

• WHERE •

On the southeastern tip of the national park.

• WHEN TO VISIT •

Ranger-assisted tours into Cliff Palace are available May through late October (months subject to change). The park is open year-round, and views of the dwelling from Cliff Palace Overlook can be experienced during low season. December brings the holiday Luminaria Festival, when Cliff Palace twinkles with the lights of golden luminarias (lanterns inside of paper bags).

• HOW TO GET THERE •

Once you reach the park entrance, stop at the Far View Visitor Center for information before driving an hour down the park road to Cliff Palace Overlook, where you can look down on the dwelling or join a ranger-assisted tour.

Mesa Top Loop Road and Wetherill Mesa Road

CO

Your Must-See Guide

With hundreds of dwellings and thousands of archaeological sites scattered throughout Mesa Verde, you can plan on seeing many incredible landmarks during your time there. One of the easiest ways to maximize your experience is by exploring the park along scenic drives, stopping wherever you can to immerse yourself in a fascinating cultural history.

The park has two auto-touring roads that skirt the rims of Navajo Canyon. The more popular of the two is the six-mile Mesa Top Loop Road in the Chapin Mesa area where you can join ranger-led tours into significant Ancestral Puebloan dwellings such as Cliff Palace, step onto overlooks peering over ancient villages like Square Tower House, and explore at your own pace on short trails to twelve surface archaeological sites. Downloading and listening to the audio tour along the way is a must; this allows you to gain a better understanding of all you are seeing.

After experiencing Mesa Top Loop Road, venture to the twelve-mile Wetherill Mesa Road on the opposite side of the canyon. There are sharper turns and steeper grades on this road and fewer dwellings to see, which results in less traffic and therefore a more intimate

THE ANCESTRAL PUEBLO PEOPLE

Due to the height of the dwellings, many have wondered about how tall the people that once lived there might have been. It is estimated that an average man of the time would have been about five foot four to five foot five, and the average woman about five foot to five foot one. While this seems on the small side compared to present populations, if you look at the size of the average European during this same time period, they were approximately the same stature. The Ancestral Pueblo people also didn't have a very long life span, usually living only to about age thirty-two to thirty-four.

experience with the ancient landscape. Look for Badger House on the surface of the plateau, Step House (self-guided), and Long House (guided tour only).

On either roadway, keep your eyes out for wildlife like deer, elk, bobcat, badgers, and birds, of which more than two hundred species have been documented in the park!

Downloading and listening to the audio tour along the way is a must; this allows you to gain a better understanding of all you are seeing.

• WHAT •

Two self-guided auto-touring roads among ancient cliff dwellings and ancestral ruins.

• WHERE •

On the park's west side running north-south on both sides of Navajo Canyon.

• WHEN TO VISIT •

April through mid-June and mid-August through mid-October are great times of year when weather is warm but not sweltering and roads are less congested with summer travelers. Mesa Top Loop Road is open year-round. Wetherill Mesa Road is open May through September, weather permitting.

• HOW TO GET THERE •

Start at the Mesa Verde Visitor and Research Center and drive just under forty-five minutes along the main park road to the fork at the Far View area, where you can cut left for Mesa Top Loop Road or right to Wetherill Mesa Road.

Rainbow Forest Museum and Giant Logs Trail

AZ

Your Must-See Guide

This stop is a two-for-one connecting an educational experience at the Rainbow Forest Museum and an exploratory one outside of it along the Giant Logs Trail.

The museum serves up a taste of the natural history of the Petrified Forest, providing background on the origins of the petrified wood alongside comprehensive exhibits that describe the area's prehistoric past, including fossils of dinosaurs and animals that once roamed the region. It is also a visitor center where you can obtain practical information about where to go and what to see and do in the park, inquire about backcountry permits, and learn why this area has the park's highest concentration of petrified wood.

Behind the museum is a short, half-mile hike on the Giant Logs Trail where along the paved pathway you are surrounded by some of the largest and most vibrantly colored logs in the park, along with small pieces that have been carved off and scattered by strong winds that the high-plateau area of Arizona is known for. This could possibly be the most interesting gravel-like landscape you've ever seen. Be sure not to miss the largest piece of petrified wood in the national park, called "Old Faithful."

The beauty of this stop is that you can gather insight to inform your trip and see a lot of natural wonders along the way. Whether you are in and out in under an hour or stay the

A FOREST THAT ISN'T A FOREST

The petrified forests aren't actually forests; they are more like petrified logjams in an ancient riverbed. Long ago, the trees fell into a river and became buried beneath mud, sand, silt, and volcanic ash. As time passed, the minerals began to seep into the wood. Eventually, the mineral material bonded with the tree cells and replaced them. Now the trees are no longer wood but stone.

better part of the day, you are free to move as the wind blows you!

 Park Snapshot

If you are looking for wind-sculpted landscapes, winding trails speckled with crystalized ancient trees, and rugged wide-open space—Petrified Forest is the place.

Glinting across the arid grasslands, you will find large deposits of prehistoric petrified wood. On the outside, the hearty bark appears like that of any old-growth tree, but when you touch it, it is as hard and smooth as stone. Inside is ornately designed quartz that shows a kaleidoscope of colorful crystal with every shift of the sunlight.

Beneath the landscape that cradles the petrified wood is a vast swatch of land—areas like the Painted Desert in the north section stretching all the way from the Grand Canyon, resting like a sunset painted onto contoured clay and mudstone. Rock art and dwellings that describe a primitive human history dot the landscape, providing a glimpse into earlier times in the area that is now the national park.

• WHAT •

An introduction to the ancient landscape along a short loop hike, with an informational stop at a visitor center/museum to cap it off.

• WHERE •

Near the south entrance of the park, off US-180.

• WHEN TO VISIT •

May through late September is the busiest time of year. July and August are the hottest months, which can bring wild weather and thunderstorms that could interrupt certain experiences. April and May are the best times to see the desert wildflowers bloom.

• HOW TO GET THERE •

Drive two miles from the south park entrance or twenty-six miles from the north park entrance to the Rainbow Forest Museum; after enjoying a visit inside, head to the backyard to enjoy the short immersive trail.

AZ

Blue Mesa

Your Must-See Guide

While a lot of trails in the national park fall on flat ground, Blue Mesa enfolds you with purple, blue, gray, peach, and ivory sculpted hillsides that nestle you within them. The colors are a result of manganese, iron, and other minerals and sediment reacting to exposure to wind and water. In the nook of the cascading bentonite clay formations lie toppled pieces of petrified wood that haven't moved for eons apart from the short distances the winds have pushed them.

CHECK OUT THE NIGHT SKY

The low level of light pollution in the area allows for a canopy of shimmering stars overhead all year long. The International Dark Sky Park is an excellent spot to gaze at the night sky while backpacking, during ranger-led night walks, and on photo expeditions led by the Petrified Forest Field Institute.

The only way to see Blue Mesa besides from a flightseeing tour soaring above or from viewpoints along the five-mile Blue Mesa Scenic Road is to walk into it—down a meandering one-mile loop trail alternating between paved and dirt pathways (with steep hikes into the canyon and back up to the trailhead). Exploring there during the dawn and dusk hours provides soft, warm light and is typically the best time of day to take photographs. When there is cloud cover, and after a rain, even bolder colors of the mesa are revealed and make for perfect picture-taking.

Blue Mesa is a long-studied research and scientific investigation site where paleontologists have found hoards of plant and animal fossils and specimens in the depths of the layered clay and mud earth. It is also a favorite site of the National Park Service rangers and of visitors who want to experience something completely unique to all other areas in the park.

Exploring there during the dawn and dusk hours provides soft, warm light and is typically the best time of day to take photographs. When there is cloud cover, and after a rain, even bolder colors of the mesa are revealed.

• WHAT •

Colorful badlands toppled with petrified wood deposits; part of the Painted Desert and the Chinle Formation.

• WHERE •

On a spur road at the halfway point of the main park road that runs north to south.

• WHEN TO VISIT •

March through October is generally considered the best window of time to visit. July through September brings monsoons and, along with them, dramatic skies and water that color the landscape. February through May has temperate weather and fewer people, though it may be windy.

• HOW TO GET THERE •

Start from the Painted Desert Visitor Center in the north or the Rainbow Forest Museum in the south and drive ten miles to the Blue Mesa sun shelter trailhead parking area, where you can start the trail.

Trail Ridge Road

CO

Your Must-See Guide

Trail Ridge Road is one of the most prized scenic byways ever constructed and is a must-explore in the national park! The road is entirely paved along forty-eight miles connecting one side of the park to the other, coursing through a diverse range of natural ecosystems—from grassy lowlands to subalpine fir and spruce forests to the apex above the tree line, where alpine tundra, big skies, and even bigger views dominate the area. Along the way, there are plenty of trails to explore, including pullouts at spectacular viewpoints that peer across the snow-dusted Rockies. You can count on wildlife sightings, so plan for a full day (and more, if you have the time).

The road's east side near Estes Park is a rich habitat for elk and aspen trees that burst into golden color during autumn leaf-peeping season. As you go farther up—ascending four thousand feet in a short amount of time—you might spot bighorn sheep while making your way to the highest point of the road, topping out at 12,183 feet. Not far beyond this point is the Alpine Visitor Center, a popular stop for information and refreshments and the road's unofficial halfway point.

On the west side near Grand Lake, stop at Milner Pass for a photo op of the Continental Divide site marker and sign post, and keep your eyes peeled for moose munching on vegetation. From Farview Curve in the scenic Kawuneeche Valley, you can see the source waters of the Colorado River—which cuts all the way to the Grand Canyon in Arizona.

KNOW BEFORE YOU GO

Due to the high elevation and mountainous terrain, Trail Ridge Road might close temporarily at times during May, June, and October due to snowfall. Check for closures and road conditions on the official National Park Service website before heading out on your trip. Reservations for timed entry may be required.

🛡 Park Snapshot

There is no denying the adoration for Rocky Mountain National Park among wilderness lovers from all over the globe. Just seventy miles northwest of Denver, the complex ecosystem contains some of the best qualities that any national park has to offer: lush lowlands, alpine forests, crystal lakes, glaciers, and snowcapped mountain peaks that together climb through the sky between 8,000 and 14,259 feet.

Once you get your bearings on life in high altitudes, adventures can be low-key with leisurely strolls on paved walkways along pristine reflective lakes, scenic drives where wildlife viewing is top-notch, and easy day hikes in a perfect wilderness. Cycling, horseback riding, photography, and other excursions are available in this world-class adventure park that is a true wilderness playground. And, of course, the glacier-capped trails beckon mountaineers, backpackers, and climbers who really want to get in it while standing up to a mile above Denver, known as the "Mile High City."

• WHAT •

The highest continuous paved road in the United States and one of America's most prized scenic byways. The road connects two sides of the park, Estes Park to the east and Grand Lake to the west, rising to the sky at its highest point, 12,183 feet above sea level.

• WHERE •

Cutting through the heart of the Rocky Mountains in the central part of the national park.

• WHEN TO VISIT •

Late May through mid-October when the road is open (closures can occur due to weather).

• HOW TO GET THERE •

From Estes Park, start at the Fall River entrance. From the Grand Lake entrance, start at the Kawuneeche Visitor Center. Trail Ridge Road follows the spine of the carved mountain from one point to the other, running east/west through the park.

Bear Lake Nature Trail

CO

Your Must-See Guide

Rocky Mountain National Park is known for its pristine reflective lakes; deep-green spruce, pine, and fir forests; and, of course, the magnificent Rocky Mountains that rise high over the landscape. At Bear Lake, you can see all these sights in one perfect, picturesque scene while hitting one of the most lauded points of interest in the park at the same time.

While this national park has no shortage of big adventure, sometimes you want to take it easy, and the just-over-half-mile interpretive trail that circles the lake allows for just that. There are thirty stops marked on the interpretive trail guide found at the start of the loop that detail stories about the area's natural and human history—follow the path in a counterclockwise direction to match the guide points. In the distance, and reflected in the lake waters on a still day, you can marvel at the magnitude of Hallett Peak and the Continental Divide with views of Longs Peak—the park's highest peak standing 14,259 feet above sea level—in the distance to the south.

On the shores, debris from grounded trees provides a playground for scampering squirrels and chipmunks. You may see deer or elk wandering among the forested areas, as well as native species of birds such as Steller's jays and nutcrackers that dress the environment with birdsong.

Whether your journey starts and ends at the lake, or you choose to build on your adventure by heading off from the area onto bigger trails, you can't go wrong at Bear Lake!

PARKING TIP

Finding a parking spot at this popular location can be nearly impossible during busy times of the year, midday, and on weekends. To avoid the hassle, use the free park shuttle during peak season, which you can hop on and off of at various points along Bear Lake Road.

You may see deer or elk wandering among the forested areas, as well as native species of birds such as Steller's jays and nutcrackers that dress the environment with birdsong.

• WHAT •

A picturesque alpine lake that is one of the most visited and photographed scenes in the national park, surrounded by a relatively easy dirt walking path.

• WHERE •

Eleven miles from the Beaver Meadows Visitor Center on the east side of the park.

• WHEN TO VISIT •

March through November. Visits during the early morning can be rewarding, with fewer crowds and more reflection on the lake water during calm morning weather.

• HOW TO GET THERE •

Start at the Beaver Meadows Entrance Station and turn onto the well-marked Bear Lake Road. Travel for eight and a half miles to the parking lot, looking for elk and deer that are common in the area along the way. The lake is a half mile from the parking lot.

Desert Discovery Nature Trail

AZ

Your Must-See Guide

This half-mile loop trail offers one of the best samplings of several things visitors come to this park to see: the iconic saguaro cactus, desert vegetation, and beautiful scenery in the American Southwest. Wandering through a maze of saguaros on a well-maintained pathway, visitors of all ages and abilities are in for an easy-breezy outing with fascinating features at all eye levels.

This is a place where you can really get to know Saguaro's biodiversity. Interpretive signs mark the loop, noting different kinds of cacti (saguaro, cholla, and prickly pear) as well as desert succulents, trees, and shrubs. Signage also describes the unique animals and birds that have adapted to the scarcity of water and extreme temperatures in the region. The large saguaro cacti standing tall above you and strewn across the landscape are some of the oldest in the region. While humans marvel at the size, shape, and individuality of these treelike plants, animals rely on them as an important food source. Birds rely on them for protection from the elements, nesting in cavities of the cacti flesh before abandoning them to be used by other birds.

This is a fantastic place to capture photographs of desert flora and fauna, especially when there are blooms on full display. It is also a good starter hike to get a lay of the land before heading out onto longer trails in Saguaro West, such as the Wild Dog Trail (just under two miles) and the King Canyon and Gould

THE SAGUARO CACTUS

The saguaro cactus (pronounced sah-wah-roh) is the largest cactus in the United States. It can normally reach about forty feet high, but some have grown as tall as seventy-eight feet. Some saguaros have dozens of "arms," while others never produce any. Though the saguaro cactus has become a symbol of the American West, it only grows in the Sonoran Desert.

Mine Loop Trail (just under two and a half miles).

 Park Snapshot

Saguaro is split between two national park sections that lie on either side of the city of Tucson. Saguaro West has a higher concentration of saguaro trees, is more open, and is the most visited area. This is where you can immerse yourself in a different kind of forest—featuring a symbol depicting the US Southwest desert unlike any other. As if celebrating, the prickly green cactus stands tall, with two arms outstretching to touch the sky. Some are perfect-looking; some are mangled; and some are large or incredibly old—all are important to the ecosystem of desert wildlife and birdlife that make their home in the Sonora Desert.

Saguaro East has elevations ranging from 2,670 feet to 8,666 feet, where mixed wood and conifer forests invite greater plant and wildlife biodiversity to the rugged landscape. It is larger, older, and more secluded than Saguaro West and is enchanting in its uniqueness.

• WHAT •

An interpretive pathway that wanders along saguaro cactus, vegetation, and desert scrub brush.

• WHERE •

One mile north of the Red Hills Visitor Center in the Tucson Mountain District in the east area of the park.

• WHEN TO VISIT •

March through May and September through November are the two peak visitor seasons in Saguaro, when the spring wildflowers bloom and weather is most comfortable. Sunrise and sunset are particularly stunning times of day along this trail, as the shape of the saguaro cactus contrasts boldly against the burning orange sun that gives way to softly colored desert skies.

• HOW TO GET THERE •

Turn onto Kinney Road and follow it two miles to the Red Hills Visitor Center, then continue one mile more to the parking area.

AZ

Cactus Forest Loop Drive

Your Must-See Guide

Get ready to roll down your windows and take your time on this paved eight-mile road that crosses through some of the most diverse desert wilderness you have ever laid eyes on. Large cacti including the saguaro and cholla are two of the most notable of the area, though you will be struck by the variety of vegetation that crawls along the desert floor. Also crawling through the landscape is fascinating wildlife that you may or may not see—lizards darting across rocky terrain, the Arizona mountain kingsnake, black bear, and countless bird species including

NAVIGATION TIP

It is recommended by the Park Service at Saguaro not to rely on mobile mapping apps, as they tend to confuse the two districts, which are located about thirty miles apart. Plan to enter the address of your exact destination to find your way with the help of your GPS or mobile device.

the Mexican spotted owl. Also living there and extremely rare to see is the fabled Gila monster, North America's only venomous lizard.

The one-way loop road and bike path are as beloved to road bikers as they are to hikers, horseback trail riders, and auto-explorers who want to experience the wilds of the Sonoran Desert. Pull-offs abound along the route, where you can stop and wander to overlooks that peer over the valley with views of the sweeping preserve and its surrounding mountains that climb to nearly nine thousand feet at the top of Mica Mountain. There are also picnic areas as well as several short interpretive trails.

This drive closes when the sun goes down, and visiting hours are enforced by the Park Service. If you wish to linger into the night, plan to join a ranger-led night program for astral-viewing through telescopes that gaze into the solar system and universe.

Pull-offs abound along the route, where you can stop and wander to overlooks that peer over the valley with views of the sweeping preserve and its surrounding mountains that climb to nearly nine thousand feet at the top of Mica Mountain.

Dunes Drive

NM

Your Must-See Guide

Dunes Drive is exactly what it sounds like: a passageway into White Sands' powdery white gypsum dune fields. The first five miles are paved, and the last three are packed sand. Beyond the roadway, the vast landscape glitters and rolls into the distance with shifting shadow and light decorating the fields beneath a blue-sky backdrop. Along the sixteen-mile out-and-back journey, desert scrublands give way to sprawling dunes that can easily be mistaken for billowing mounds of snow.

CHECK FOR CLOSURES

The national park is surrounded by the White Sands Missile Range, which conducts military tests throughout the year. Testing requires area closures for visitor safety, including on Dunes Drive, for durations of up to three hours. The White Sands National Park Visitor Center and gift shop remain open to visitors during closures.

Pullouts line the perimeter leading to marked hiking trails, picnic areas, and outdoor exhibits that teach you about the Chihuahuan Desert, the national park's long history as a national monument, and drought-resistant desert plants that are now well matched with the arid environment. You will also learn about cool desert wildlife that you might encounter during your visit, such as coyotes, foxes, bobcats, badgers, and porcupines.

This drive is as much about its access points as it is about the scenery. The roadway is a jumping-off point to both easy and moderate trails on wooden boardwalk, dry lake bed, and flat sand, and onto the larger dunes where, in designated areas, you can head out for a fun-filled adventure sandboarding their soft slopes. Dunes Drive is a go-to spot for nature and landscape photographers who are gifted with an always changing landscape and weather systems that add interest to the scenery, where desert succulents and yucca plants spot the landscape in unique and picturesque ways, blooming from late May through June.

Park Snapshot

Across two hundred and seventy-five square miles of desert in southern New Mexico, a sea of glistening sand lies across a unique natural landscape rippling like an ocean, wherein every fine grain the secrets of an ancient world that once existed there remain. The gypsum sand forming the famed dunes has proliferated in the Tularosa Basin due to the dry climate and unique weather patterns. In other areas of the park, you'll find varying microclimates—such as Lake Lucero, which, during monsoon season, holds water that serves up reflections of the sky, and desert-adapted plants and animals that remarkably thrive in the rugged terrain. This is a great adventure park too. Whether you want to hike easy or strenuous trails, ride horseback, camp in the backcountry (when access is available), or share a belly laugh with others while sliding gleefully down rare mineral fields—there are boundless ways to have fun in this park.

• WHAT •

A scenic drive in the heart of the world's largest gypsum dune field on the only established roadway in the national park.

• WHERE •

In the northeast area of the national park.

• WHEN TO VISIT •

March through April or early May, before the sweltering summer heat and storm season set in. September through November is a favorable time to visit in terms of milder weather, though wind gusts might spray you with sand unexpectedly (which could really happen at any time of year). There is road maintenance year-round and almost daily along Dunes Drive to clear the roadway of sand drifts.

• HOW TO GET THERE •

US Route 70 leads to the park visitor center, from where you can get info before starting your adventure on Dunes Drive.

Old Faithful

Your Must-See Guide

Old Faithful might be one of the most famous landmarks of any national park, and it is without a doubt the most well-known geyser in the world. Every one to two hours, it sends just-under-200°F water more than one hundred feet skyward for durations lasting anywhere from one to fifteen minutes—which it has predictably done ever since tracking began in 1870. No wonder it is called "Old Faithful"!

With such consistency, you can be sure that anytime you go, the next eruption is not long after your arrival. If this site is at the top of your list, a favorite place to stay is at the historic Old Faithful Inn, from where you can step outside to the viewing platforms in a matter of minutes. The inn, cited as the largest cabin-style lodge structure in the world, was built in 1903 to 1904 and is a National Historic Landmark.

If you are staying elsewhere in the park, have no fear—parking spots in adjacent lots are plentiful and just a short walk to viewing sites where you can see activity that occurs throughout the day and night.

There are three main viewing locations for the Old Faithful geyser: from inside Old Faithful Lodge, from Observation Point (reachable on a short one-mile out-and-back trail), and on the boardwalk viewing platform. The boardwalk is the most popular place to view, so plan to arrive soon after the most recent activity to grab yourself a good spot.

INSIDER TIP

America's oldest national park bisects three states, with the bulk of it residing in Wyoming, and with special areas crossing two northern boundary states—where you can experience celebrated sites such as the grand rock entrance gate located in Gardiner, Montana (the park's only entrance open year-round).

Park Snapshot

Yellowstone was the first US national park, designated for preservation in 1872 after its fanciful environment captured the attention of explorers, artists, and eventually lawmakers. The landscape enfolds more than half of Earth's geothermal features—a diverse collection of geysers, mud pots, fumaroles, and hot springs that brim and bubble beneath your feet. The geothermal activity is just one of Yellowstone's biggest draws; visitors are also attracted to the wildlife that graces the expansive forests, hillsides, and valleys crossing more than two million surface acres. On scenic drives and treks into the park, you can see bison, bears, and gray wolves, and the wildlife viewing doesn't stop there—Yellowstone has the largest concentration of wildlife in the lower forty-eight states. And where there is wildlife, there is water. The Yellowstone River, a popular destination for fly-fishing, starts in the valley and flows eastward all the way to the Atlantic Ocean.

• WHAT •

The most consistently running, most famous geyser on Earth, and the first geyser in the park to be named. Few go to Yellowstone without seeing Old Faithful!

• WHERE •

In the southwest area of the park in the Old Faithful Historic District in the Upper Geyser Basin.

• WHEN TO VISIT •

All seasons are popular at Yellowstone. Summer is the most visited; spring and fall are particularly great with fewer crowds and pleasant weather. Winter visits can provide a more intimate and unusual experience.

• HOW TO GET THERE •

Drive south or east on Grand Loop Road (Route 89) and follow the clearly marked signage to the Old Faithful turnoff to the Old Faithful Visitor and Education Center, where there is designated parking.

Artist Point

Your Must-See Guide

The Grand Canyon of the Yellowstone is sometimes credited as the reason Yellowstone was established as a national park, with artistic renditions capturing its beauty during early expeditions that inspired federal lawmakers. It can be enjoyed from many viewpoints on both the North and South Rims, though the view from Artist Point is the most famous. One look, and you will see why! With evergreen pine trees blanketing the colorful canyon walls and a rushing waterfall cutting through the heart of the vista,

you almost can't believe that so much beauty can be contained in one area. If your intent is to enjoy a peaceful scene or capture a show-stopping photograph, head there in the early part of the day—sunrise is best—to see the scene in warm light and possibly a rainbow produced by the sunshine casting down on the flowing water. During the summer, butterflies and birdlife fly through the skies, including bald eagles, ravens, and osprey that nest in the Canyon Village area of the park.

From the main viewpoint, wander along the South Rim to Point Sublime to take it all in from a different vantage point. Look for wildlife on the way—Yellowstone is home to many large animals including bison, deer, elk, and black bear. A trip to this area could be as short as an hour if you're just checking out the view, or you could linger a full day to hike the perimeter areas where the views will continue to stop you in your tracks.

ADVENTURE SAFELY!

You're likely to encounter wildlife at Yellowstone, and any animal's behavior can be unpredictable, especially if you have a meeting while on foot. Head to the National Park Service website and to the park visitor center to learn about area wildlife and techniques that can help keep you safe while exploring.

During the summer, butterflies and birdlife fly through the skies, including bald eagles, ravens, and osprey that nest in the Canyon Village area of the park.

A viewpoint looking onto the South Rim of the Grand Canyon of the Yellowstone and the lower Yellowstone Falls pouring onto the scene.

• WHERE •

In the central area of the park, on the South Rim of the Grand Canyon of the Yellowstone.

• WHEN TO VISIT •

June through August are the most popular months; April to early June, September, and October bring great weather and fewer crowds.

• HOW TO GET THERE •

Drive from Canyon Junction where Norris Canyon Road and Grand Loop Road converge and continue two miles to South Rim Drive. The viewpoint is located just a short walk from a large parking lot. You can also hike there along the South Ridge Trail, which starts at Uncle Tom's Trail parking lot.

The Narrows

Your Must-See Guide

The Narrows Trail in Zion is a one-of-a-kind trail and is a coveted one in terms of experiencing the very best that Zion has to offer. There are several ways to experience The Narrows—such as heading out to Riverside Walk on a one-mile dry and paved pathway alongside the river or traveling through it—the preferred way to explore this trail and what makes it so exciting.

Sloshing through the Virgin River with trekking poles keeping

you upright against the current, you are bound to feel like a great explorer as you travel through a seemingly hidden canyon where the scenery is next level. Outfitted in water-repellent gear or a dry suit, you will head out on a pathway of flowing water and river rock beneath your boots as you make your way through an enclave of limestone and Navajo sandstone walls that tower one thousand feet above your head. In some sections, the river-bed stretches only twenty to thirty feet. You can journey in for a short amount of time and turn back, or immerse yourself fully in the environment on a ten-mile round-trip hike to Big Spring, which is moderately strenuous because you will be wading through water the entire way. There is also a sixteen-mile trail that requires preparation, endurance, and time and is wholly rewarding. To prepare for any adventure at The Narrows, head to the town of Springdale outside the southern edge of the park, where you can get

WATCH FOR FLASH FLOODS

Flash floods can and do happen in The Narrows following heavy rainfall in the North Fork. The river can rise from eighteen inches to six feet in minutes, making travel impossible and sometimes deadly. Always check the weather before hiking The Narrows, and inquire with the National Park Service rangers at Zion about the possibility of weather-related closures.

wilderness permits, rent gear, and trail information.

Park Snapshot

From dramatic cliffs rising two thousand feet above the Zion Valley to the ultra-green Virgin River that cuts through them, it is no wonder Zion is a favorite among national park-goers. Such an environment creates a fun place to explore, while preserving a healthy habitat for wildlife and vegetation. That eco-system stretches from the main canyon area in the south to the remote Kolob Terrace area and Kolob Canyons in the north, where you are more likely to see wildlife and where world-class backcountry wilderness trails and backpacking adventures await. In the main canyon, access to trails, points of interest, and sweeping views are made easy along the twenty-five-mile Zion Mount Carmel Highway and Tunnel, a National Historic Civil Engineering Landmark.

From just one look at the canyons, verdant valleys, and coursing waterways, you will see why Native Americans, settlers, and avid park fans have called this the most majestic land of all.

• WHAT •

An inner-canyon hiking trail with the Virgin River as the pathway.

• WHERE •

In the northeast section of the main area of the national park, at the North Fork of the Virgin River (the narrowest section of Zion Canyon).

• WHEN TO VISIT •

June, July, September, and October, when the water is warmest and the water level is at its lowest. Note that The Narrows closes on occasion during the summer months when flash floods run through the canyon. This could be life-threatening for hikers.

• HOW TO GET THERE •

Start at the Temple of Sinawava via the Riverside Walk, hiking back the same route (wilderness permit not required), or start at the Chamberlain's Ranch Trailhead to the Temple of Sinawava (wilderness permit/drop-off transportation required).

Angel's Landing and the West Rim Trail

UT

Your Must-See Guide

If you ask any traveler headed to Zion National Park what trails are on their itinerary, you can expect that a day spent exploring Angel's Landing and the West Rim Trail is on the list. This is *the* classic Zion hike and is a well-known trail to experienced hikers.

The first four miles lead to Scout Lookout, where views of the valley sprawl in all directions and where you can perform a gut check to determine whether hiking the last leg of the trail to Angel's Landing is for you. The one-mile climb from Scout to Angel's Landing traces a narrow, exposed canyon spine with support chains to guide you to the main lookout. There are typically many hikers on the trail but when you get to the top at fifteen hundred feet, you'll feel like it is just you and what feels like all of Utah.

If you are not interested in this kind of adrenalin rush, there is no shame in opting out of a summit to Angel's Landing. There will be plenty of other hikers who didn't want to venture onto the high peak parked on boulders nearby at Scout Lookout. If you are resting there, you have already hiked switchbacks offering really cool photo opportunities of the valley floor on terrain that is both challenging and satisfying to no end. And the views from Scout Lookout are incredible too.

HAVE YOUR PERMIT

Starting in 2022, permits are required to hike to the top of Angel's Landing in response to concerns about trail congestion on the narrow sky-high trail. Rangers may request to see your permit, so be sure to have it on you. They are issued through two different lotteries on www.recreation.gov.

There are typically many hikers on the trail but when you get to the top at fifteen hundred feet, you'll feel like it is just you and what feels like all of Utah.

One of the most popular trails in the country, with challenging hiking and sweeping views from the top of the trail.

Zion Canyon, in the south section of the park.

March through October. Summer brings storms that can make hiking on the slickrock dangerous; weather is the mildest in the spring and fall.

At the Zion National Park Visitor Center, park and walk to the Zion Canyon Shuttle System pickup and ride the shuttle to the Grotto Trailhead at stop 6. The trailhead is on Zion Canyon Scenic Drive, which is closed to private vehicles when shuttles are in service (March through November); you can drive to the parking area during the winter season.

CHAPTER 3

Island Parks Region

HI

Haleakalā Crater Summit and Sliding Sands Trail

Your Must-See Guide

The Haleakalā Crater Summit area brings you to the rooftop of Maui, where you can stand above the clouds and on a surreal volcanic area that locals call the "House of the Sun." At sunrise, morning light bursts onto the scene, illuminating a sea of clouds that eventually breaks to reveal a deeply colored cinder cone landscape leading far into the distance. On a clear morning, you can see the islands of Lanai, Molokai, and Hawaii Island (commonly referred to as the "Big Island").

Witnessing this scene at this time of day is a commitment. You'll need to head out in the predawn hours to position yourself in time to see first light. For most, it is worth every second of lost sleep—and after witnessing a scene so magical, you will be wide awake and ready to take on more adventure. If you can venture onward along a meandering crater hike, head from the summit down the Sliding Sands Trail for eleven miles of hiking bliss. Traversing a rainbow-strewn landscape, you will walk aside endangered silversword plants that glow beneath the tropical sunshine, and, farther into the crater, you are sure to see endangered Hawaiian geese (called nēnē), making this truly a one-of-a-kind experience!

If you prefer to see the summit when you are better rested, evening is a lovely time to enjoy a Hawaiian sunset from the unique vantage point atop Maui's crater rim. At nightfall, starry skies emerge to reveal the cosmos and, on occasion, rare astrological events such as halos and moonbows.

PLAN AHEAD

Advanced reservations are required to enter the Crater Summit parking lot between the hours of 3:00 a.m. and 7:00 a.m. Pacific time, so plan to book a reservation before your sunrise trip there, which can be done on www.recreation.gov up to sixty days in advance of your visit.

Park Snapshot

If you want to experience Maui's wild nature, Haleakalā is the place. Here, you can meet the morning sky and travel to the coastal shores that Hawaii is famous for in the space of one day.

The Haleakalā Crater Summit towers above Maui at its highest point and is where, according to legend, the demigod Maui ensnared the sun to gather more daylight for the island. From the top of the crater, a scenic drive along the Hana Highway travels thirty-eight miles of lush rainforest canopies to the shores of the Kīpahulu coastal region where black sand beaches and aquamarine waters await. You will experience several microclimates along the way, ranging from rugged high-elevation volcanic scrubland and dry forest zones to emerald-green slopes that are brought to life by waterfalls. Colorful tropical wildflowers and birdlife seem to guide you from one adventure to the next, like unofficial trail markers leading the way.

• WHAT •

The highest point on the island standing 10,023 feet above sea level.

• WHERE •

In the south-central part of the island, on the west side of the national park.

• WHEN TO VISIT •

April, May, and October through January have the most predictable weather, which is warm and mostly mild. The summit temperature is on average 30 percent cooler than the coastal areas, so layer up and plan to shed as you descend the trail if you choose to add that to your summit trip.

• HOW TO GET THERE •

Start the two-hour drive up the Haleakalā Highway (HI-37) around 3:00 a.m. Pacific time to get to the summit parking lot before sunrise. Plan to stay in your car to keep warm until dawn, then head out to the viewpoint, which is a short walk away.

HI

Kīpahulu District

Your Must-See Guide

Whether you travel the famous fifty-four-mile Road to Hana from the summit area of the park or drive the south coast state highway that is preferred by locals, a journey into the Kīpahulu area will capture any nature lover's heart. This is classic Hawaii landscape, with technicolor green rainforests in inland areas and where surfers ride swells off the seacoast. It is also the beating heart of the island for protected native Hawaiian culture (a stop at the local bread stands in Keʻanae is a must!).

Along the Road to Hana, the Pools of Oheo (Seven Sacred Pools) is a popular stop, with waters flowing through the trees as they make their way to the Pacific Ocean. If you do miss this stop, there are scores of other falls where you can cool off and explore the rainforest canopies during breaks along your drive. Once you've reached Kīpahulu, head to the visitor center to get info before starting a four-mile out-and-back hike along the Pipiwai Trail that leads through dense vegetation—a rich habitat for birds and insects. This trail leads to incredible sights, such as a massive banyan tree and eventually a bamboo forest where all you will see is clean, green, wild Hawaiian nature in every direction.

When you are done in the trees, head to the beach. Waiʻanapanapa Beach is lined by a black sand shoreline that cradles sea caves, blowholes, and a natural sea arch—all kissed by the breath of salty sea air from the Pacific Ocean.

THE ROAD TO HANA

The best tool you can carry on your drive along the Road to Hana is patience. There are fifty-nine one-lane bridges and six hundred and twenty curves slowing the course, and the structure is unlikely to change, as locals are determined to keep the historic character of the scenic road intact.

The Pipiwai Trail leads through dense vegetation—a rich habitat for birds and insects. This trail leads to incredible sights, such as a massive banyan tree and eventually a bamboo forest where all you will see is clean, green, wild Hawaiian nature in every direction.

An oasis of lush tropical rainforest perched upon coastal waters and an important area of protection for native Hawaiian land.

In the southeast area of the park; on the southeast part of the island of Maui.

April through May and September through November—outside of the rainy summer season (and the winter tourist season when the island is most crowded).

This really depends on where you are coming from. The fabled Road to Hana (Hana Highway) begins at mile marker 0 in the town of Kahului before traveling along the northeast coast of Maui to the coastal Kīpahulu area (located past the town of Hana). You can also drive on the south edge of the island along Highway 31.

HI

Crater Rim Drive

Your Must-See Guide

If you are ready for a classic Volcanoes National Park experience, hop in the car, roll down your windows, and head out on a self-guided auto-tour of Crater Rim Drive, skirting the edge of the Kīlauea Caldera. Along eleven miles of a two-lane paved roadway, a magical landscape crossing rainforest and desert ecosystems enfolds you—filled with curious features such as large craters, steam vents, volcanos (of course), as well as cool wildlife and tropical birds and plant life.

While you can complete this drive in about forty-five minutes,

GET INFO UPON ARRIVAL

A stop at the visitor center is a must to get up-to-date information on volcanic activity and related road and trail closures and to learn what the Park Service is up to in terms of activities during your time there. Ask for info about where to see cool wildlife in the park.

plan for a longer excursion, as there are many ways to venture off on foot from the scenic road and viewpoints. A favorite first stop is at the Kīlauea Overlook where dramatic views of the Halemaʻumaʻu Crater (Kīlauea's main crater) are punctuated by blue-colored steam billowing into the sky. If the crater erupts at night, you'll see fiery orange lava glowing against a black landscape.

While much of Hawaii is fragrant with the scent of tropical flowers, the air at Volcanoes carries a strong scent of pungent sulfur. It is especially strong on the Halemaʻumaʻu (Sulphur Banks) paved trail, where sulfuric crystal deposits lie beside the boardwalk. The Kīlauea Iki Overlook peers onto a large crater that once held a lake of lava. At Wahinekapu (Steaming Bluff), vapor rises from steam vents in the ground. You won't want to miss the five-hundred-year-old Thurston Lava Tube (Nāhuku) with its cave-like tunnel formed by lava coursing through the landscape in the mid-twentieth century.

 Park Snapshot

Have you heard of Pele? She is the mythical Hawaiian goddess of fire, lightning, wind, and volcanoes, and, according to legend, Volcanoes' main crater is her home.

For seventy million years, volcanoes have spewed lava into the Pacific Ocean, forming a chain of islands that are as mystical in their construction as they are beautiful to the beholder. This national park gives a different type of experience than common Hawaiian vacations where travelers bask on palmy shores by day and shake their hips at luaus by night. The southeast coast of the Big Island is both raw and alive, shaped by two of the most active volcanoes on Earth: Kīlauea (4,091 feet) and Mauna Loa (13,679 feet). The geology and biology are continuously changing, with terrain just as wild aboveground as it is below Earth's crust where magma pulses to find the surface—forming a conduit between this world and Pele's ancient Hawaii.

• WHAT •

A paved scenic roadway encircling the edge of the Kīlauea Caldera, with plenty of viewpoints to stop off at along the way and hiking trails leading into the landscape.

• WHERE •

On the north side of the national park; on the north rim of the Kīlauea volcano.

• WHEN TO VISIT •

Exploring Hawaii is great year-round. Temperatures range from the high 60s to the mid-80s (Fahrenheit) throughout the year, making the weather pretty perfect anytime. There are unexpected bouts of rain and windy conditions throughout the year.

• HOW TO GET THERE •

Head into the park entrance, then stop at the Kīlauea Visitor Center on the right-hand side to get info. From there, you will begin the clockwise loop from the Kīlauea Iki Overlook.

HI

Kīlauea Iki Trail

Your Must-See Guide

The Kīlauea Iki hike is a standout experience in Volcanoes and offers some of the most diverse hiking in all of Hawaii. While the location is ancient, this area was born in its current form in the middle of the twentieth century, when a series of large eruptions from the Pu'u Pua'i cinder cone flooded the area and left a sea of molten lava four hundred feet deep that cooled and solidified into the caldera that remains today. You can still see Pu'u Pua'i steaming as you wander the landscape.

The four-mile loop trail begins in a lush tropical rainforest with native flora, singing insects, and colorful birds in its canopies before descending four hundred feet from the rim, putting your feet sturdily on the basement of the crater. All around you, steam vents percolate in the lively yet desolate environment. Tufts of greenery and small flowers sprout from cracks in the hardened lava, serving as a reminder that this dynamic ecosystem is brimming with new life as well as old. Sacred Hawaiian Ahu (cairns, or stacked rocks) guide you along the way until you reach the "bathtub ring" ascent leading back to the top of the forested crater rim where you can catch some shade after a day's exposure in the crater.

To prolong your adventure, plan to stop at the Thurston Lava Tube on your way back to the car. The short hike brings you to the main attraction with enclaves of ferns and tropical birds guiding your way from the start.

MIND THE STACKS

Ahu (stacked rocks) have cultural significance to the Hawaiian people and have been deliberately placed at Kīlauea Iki to mark trails. You should not make your own stacks, as it could confuse other hikers and impact the natural ecosystem.

All around you, steam vents percolate in the lively yet desolate environment. Tufts of greenery and small flowers sprout from cracks in the hardened lava, serving as a reminder that this dynamic ecosystem is brimming with new life as well as old.

• WHAT •

A multi-environment day hike traversing rainforest and a caldera that was formed during a massive eruption in 1959. That event sent lava 1,900 feet skyward before settling to create a molten lake of lava that has since hardened into a hike-worthy oasis. The area is now known as Kīlauea Iki ("little Kīlauea").

• WHERE •

In the northern section of the park, near the Kīlauea Visitor Center.

• WHEN TO VISIT •

Year-round! In the early mornings and on cooler days, you can beat the heat, whereas there is little if any shade on the crater floor in the midday sun.

• HOW TO GET THERE •

Take Crater Rim Drive one and a half miles from the Kīlauea Visitor Center to the Kīlauea Iki trailhead, park, and start the hike following well-marked signage.

Mount 'Alava Trail

AS

Your Must-See Guide

Trail networks traversing the island of Tutuila lead you from the north shores of the island to summit viewpoints peering across the boat-dotted Pago Pago Bay. The six-and-a-half-mile Mount 'Alava Adventure Trail is an immersive and adventurous way to get there, climbing sixteen hundred feet up steep terrain with nearly sixty ladders and almost eight hundred steps strewn across the trail helping with particularly steep sections. At the top is the Mount 'Alava Summit, where the dense rainforest environment looks upon a water world that stretches out in all directions. Once you take in the views, you'll descend steep sections to Vatia village back on shore-level land. Because hiking is more of a necessity than a pastime to Samoans, you may find yourself mostly alone on the trail, which lends an entirely unique perspective in terms of all that surrounds you (and how you'll handle your own capabilities). It will likely be hot and humid, so prepare to break a sweat and expect insects as is the norm in a tropical rainforest environment.

A stop at the visitor center to get more information is a must to get the most out of your time on Tutuila, as many of the sites are a bit scattered and online tips don't always make sense until contextualized with the area. Rangers may encourage you to use local transportation and even hitchhike to paths and roads that lead to trailheads. You'll find that local residents are kind and helpful, so don't be shy about asking for help along the way.

KNOW BEFORE YOU GO

There are no bathroom services along the trail or at the summit. There is also no water along the hike, so be sure to bring plenty with you for the full journey. Also, even on sunny days, the path and rocks can be slippery, so bring appropriate footgear. Don't forget insect repellent!

Park Snapshot

Because of its remote location far south of the equator in the Pacific Ocean, this park has many distinctions that make it a completely unique national park and travel experience, making it well worth the long journey to get there.

The national park resides on three islands: Taʻū, Ofu, and Tutuila, where you will find the capital city of Pago Pago. Taʻū is unspoiled and offers the best taste of the traditional Samoan culture. Ofu features white sandy beaches and vibrant communities of tropical marine life. At Tutuila, you will find the park headquarters and the main park visitor center and be treated to the best glimpses of modern American Samoa and all that entails (i.e., visitor services!). All three areas are home to dense tropical rainforests and the creatures that live there, including fruit bats, which are key to park protection and super fun to watch darting through the canopies.

• WHAT •

The most explored trail in the National Park of American Samoa!

• WHERE •

Tutuila Island, home to the capital of Pago Pago, along the Maugaloa Ridge in the island's inland area.

• WHEN TO VISIT •

Year-round, and wonderful whenever you visit. The dry months are between June and September, which cuts down on some of the humidity and insects that can be pesky while hiking hard trails. Crowds will be sparse any time of year due to the remote location.

• HOW TO GET THERE •

The main park visitor center is located across from the Pago Way Service Station, which you can get to with the help of hired or public transport. The Mount ʻAlava Trailhead is across the road from the Lower Sauma Ridge Trail.

Ofu Beach

AS

Your Must-See Guide

American Samoa's Ofu island is often cited as having one of the most beautiful paradise beaches in the world. There, you will find four miles of immaculate coastline with pure crystal waters and vibrant communities of marine life on one side and the mountain backdrops of Sunu'itao Peak and Piumafua looking onto the seascape on the other side. The park's remote location and low level of human impact on land and at sea have allowed coral ecosystems to flourish without bleaching (a destroyer of reef systems),

A UNIQUE PARK

The National Park of America Samoa is a kind of "rental property" and the only national park that holds that distinction. The only way the National Park Service could establish the park in Samoa was to negotiate fifty-year leases with several local villages. The deal gives villagers $600,000 a year in revenue.

making it one of the best snorkel areas in the territory and a delight for climate scientists who study the effects of human impact.

On powdery sandy shorelines beneath palm trees and adjoining rainforest, you can lie back and watch fruit bats fly with wild abandon overhead with a feeling of true escape that comes from being deep in the heart of the South Pacific.

Ofu island is connected to its neighbor Olosega by the only bridge in Manu'a—from where locals and intrepid visitors can jump thirty feet into the pristine waters below before catching the current back to the shoreline. On the island, you can't miss the National Park Visitor Center, a full-service stop for information and planning advice where friendliness is part of the package. You won't find luxuries on Ofu that you might have in tropical getaways closer to home. Part of its beauty is its seclusion, and with that, you get all that comes with it, including fewer amenities and services.

On powdery sandy shorelines beneath palm trees and adjoining rainforest, you can lie back and watch fruit bats fly with wild abandon overhead with a feeling of true escape that comes from being deep in the heart of the South Pacific.

• WHAT •

White sandy beaches with palm trees, coral beaches, and unspoiled waters. Tropical forests lining the beach are a habitat for fruit bats.

• WHERE •

Ofu-Olosega in the Manu'a Islands group, sixty miles east of Tutuila and the capital city of Pago Pago.

• WHEN TO VISIT •

Any time of year is good; you can't go wrong! Temperatures are hot year-round, making waterplay easy. The hotter, wet summer season is from October through May; the cooler and drier months are June through September.

• HOW TO GET THERE •

Fly from the capital city of Pago Pago, which touches down at the Fitiuta airport just a short walk from both the Ofu Visitor Center and Ofu Beach, or enter by boat at the harbor touching down at Faleasiu.

Trunk Bay Underwater Snorkel Trail

VI

Your Must-See Guide

Trunk Bay is hands down the most popular site in the national park, thanks to many write-ups by trusted travel publications citing it as one of the most beautiful paradise beaches in the world. Once you step onto the powdery white shores lined by crystal-blue waters, you'll quickly understand why.

Trunk Bay has another big draw apart from the beach: an underwater snorkeling trail that crosses the length of more than two hundred and twenty-five yards of coral reef on the bottom of the sea. Between three and eighteen feet below the surface, you will glide alongside colorful tropical fish and other cool creatures such as sea turtles and rays that thrive in the area. Underwater trail markers along the way teach you about the lively habitat, including the precious coral reef systems that sustain marine life there. This is one of those activities that is fun for all who love to submerge in the water and is especially fun for beginners learning how to snorkel.

Don't let your adventure stop when you complete the underwater trail. The shorelines are lined with sea grape trees and coconut palms that color and shade the beaches—and with more than a quarter mile of beach to wander on, you are free to simply enjoy being somewhere wonderful.

With visitor services like a snack bar and grill, bathrooms and showers, and gear rentals for your snorkel adventure (or bring your

HELP PROTECT CORAL REEFS WHILE EXPLORING

Chemicals from sunscreen can damage coral reefs. So can trampling on or touching them. Help protect these important ecosystems by wearing proper attire, using reef-safe sunscreen, and keeping your hands and feet away while in the water. Ask for more information at the National Park Visitor Center.

own gear if you'd like), you are pretty well set to enjoy the beach all day long once you arrive.

Park Snapshot

On the island of St. John where Virgin Islands National Park is located, 60 percent of the park is on land and the remaining 40 percent is submerged beneath the Caribbean Sea—making it a wonderful place for both land- and sea-based adventures.

The island is only nine miles long, and there are only a couple of roads crossing it, so you'll find yourself adventuring on foot as you venture into the tropical landscape—on the hillsides, in tropical forests, on the beaches, and at sea.

The national park is a multisport destination where snorkeling, paddling, and diving adventures entice visitors who love waterplay in marine waters. Onshore, there are fun hiking trails in habitats where insects, lizards, and birds scurry and flitter about. There are interesting cultural finds as well that describe a human history—from ancient civilizations to sugar plantations from centuries past buried beneath vegetation that crawls across the island.

• WHAT •

An offshore underwater snorkel trail on one of the most popular beaches on the island of St. John.

• WHERE •

In the northwest area of the park.

• WHEN TO VISIT •

Year-round. Head out in the morning for the most marine activity in the waters and when there are fewer crowds on the trail and beach. Visits later in the day are great for afternoon snorkeling excursions capped off by oceanside sunset viewing.

• HOW TO GET THERE •

Head to the Trunk Bay beach parking lot and find a spot (or arrive by taxi to save yourself from having to find parking), then walk to the beach. The snorkeling trail begins next to a small island offshore and toward the right side.

CHAPTER 4

Midwest Region

Badlands Loop Road

SD

Your Must-See Guide

There is only one paved road in Badlands, and it can be enjoyed along thirty-nine miles of scenic roadway where twelve viewpoints and points of interest invite you to pull over and gaze across the spectacular landscape and head out onto marked and unmarked trails on foot to plan out your own adventure.

Along the drive, you will travel alongside dramatic formations of sedimentary rock deposits that have created colorful hills, canyons, buttes, and pinnacles that have eroded over the course of millions of years. The largest badland feature

in the park is the Badlands Wall (known simply as "The Wall")—an ancient barrier separating the upper and lower prairies. There is plenty of wildlife to see along the way moving through badlands and grassland habitats where birds of prey, reptiles, and amphibians emerge during spring and summer when the park bares the most water.

Fascinated by fossils? Badlands has one of the most concentrated mammal fossil beds on Earth. You can see and learn more about them on a guided hike along Fossil Exhibit Trail off Loop Road. Cedar Pass is said to hold many yet-to-be-discovered finds—if you see one, snap a picture and take it to the visitor center for a ranger to identify!

Regardless of where you start on Loop Road, make a point to stop by the Ben Reifel Visitor Center at the Northeast entrance, where you can learn about this curious place and pick up information that will be useful along your journey.

NOT SO BAD AFTER ALL

It is said that the Lakota people named this land *mako sica*, meaning "bad lands." And looking at the vast, desolate landscape, it's easy to see why. However, the erosion, wind, and water damage have created a colorful and picturesque scene that is a wonder to behold.

Park Snapshot

Exploring Badlands is a surreal experience—with fossil beds storying an ancient landscape underground and curious formations stretching as far as the eye can see across the largest mixed grass prairie in the United States. The complexity of badland formations glows in sun-drenched color during sunrise and sunset. Nestled in that land, wild beasts and delicate creatures freely roam—bison, mountain goats, bighorn sheep, prairie dogs, and the rarely seen endangered black-footed ferret.

This park is an active research area where rich fossil beds that have frozen ancient animals in layers of Earth are of ongoing study. A people's history is on full display as you learn about the Lakota people, who have called this land home far longer than its time as a national park. The park's southern unit lies entirely on tribal trust land and is managed by members of the Oglala Sioux Tribe.

• WHAT •

A scenic driving road leading to pull-offs and viewpoints across vast stretches of badland formations where wildlife sightings are common.

• WHERE •

In the North Unit, running from the northwest edge to the eastern boundary.

• WHEN TO VISIT •

April through June and September through November are considered shoulder season, when the weather is most temperate and there are fewer crowds than in the height of summer in July and August. Summer and winter temperatures are extreme—topping out above 100°F and reaching -40°F during the winter.

• HOW TO GET THERE •

Starting at either the Pinnacles entrance in the north area of the park or at the Northeast entrance on the eastern corner, follow SD 240 from one edge of the park to the other.

The Ledges Trail

OH

Your Must-See Guide

The Ledges Trail is a fantastic place to take in a lot of what makes Cuyahoga Valley so special in a short period of time: complex natural features, hidden forests, diverse ecosystems, and beautiful views of the valley. The trail travels over two miles through birch, oak, maple, and hemlock trees and along giant millions-years-old Sharon Conglomerate boulders that tower overhead. The entire area is covered with lichen, moss, ferns, and other vegetation in what feels like a magical forest.

A SHARED NATIONAL PARK

Through individual agreements made during the establishment of the national park in 2000, private dwellings reside within its boundaries, which is unusual. Serving the local community—as well as visitors, though not operated by the Park Service—are community events, railroad tours, art exhibits, small theater productions, a couple of restaurants, and golf.

This isn't one of those hikes where you head to a viewpoint only to turn back to the trailhead. It is totally immersive as you weave through corridors and slots with the ledges perched atop, beneath, and surrounding from all angles. Both detailed and full-scene views are fun to photograph, opening an aperture onto new growth that pulses against features that existed before humans walked the earth.

The Ice Box Cave Trail is an easy one-mile offshoot trail from the main Ledges Trail, where large cliffs line the pathway providing ample shade in what feels like an overgrown rock garden. Ice Box Cave itself may be closed during your visit, as ongoing efforts to protect bat populations continue. To extend your time in the area, you can take alternative routes to the Ledges Trail to lengthen your adventure, starting at the Pine Grove, Haskell Run, and Kendall Lake Trailheads.

Position yourself at the Ledges Overlook at sunset, where warm light casts down on the valley from the natural rock ledge viewing platform.

 Park Snapshot

Cuyahoga's proximity to the major cities of Akron and Cleveland can be felt along popular pathways where park visitors are joined by Ohio residents who jog, bike, and meet friends for dog walks on nature trails that abound in the national park.

There are just under one hundred and twenty-five miles of established trails of all difficulty levels on terrain ranging from woodland forest to wetlands to open grassy expanses that sprawl across the valley. Waterfalls are a big attraction at places like Brandywine Falls and Bridal Veil Falls, where cascading waters fall across ancient rock. The Ohio and Erie Canal and the Everett Covered Bridge lend a vibrant historical context to the midwestern thoroughfare that transformed trade routes in the country. One of the most popular park attractions is a train ride tracing the Cuyahoga River (translating as "crooked river" in native Mohawk), where paddlers glide the waters through Ohio's favorite urban wilderness.

• WHAT •

A plateau where striking rock formations are nestled into a hardwood forest along a great hiking trail.

• WHERE •

On the southeast side of the park.

• WHEN TO VISIT •

Spring and fall are preferred times to visit. April and May bring new growth and spring wildflowers. September and October offer a welcome cooldown from hot and humid summer months, and October is prime time for fall foliage. Winter is a fun time to play, but those months bring ice and snow to trails.

• HOW TO GET THERE •

If starting at the Hunt Farm Visitor Information Center, drive just under three miles northeast on Akron Peninsula Road before turning right on Truxell Road to the Ledges Trailhead, from where you can park and start your hike.

Ohio and Erie Canal Towpath Trail

OH

Your Must-See Guide

Outdoor adventure meets a historic past along the Towpath Trail, where twenty miles of established pathway follows remnants of the Ohio and Erie Canal (O&E), which once traveled through the Cuyahoga Valley region. The full trail extends outside of the national park boundaries along one hundred and one miles, of which some are newly completed. All year long, walkers, runners, hikers, bikers, and riders on horseback follow the Ohio and Erie Canalway, while paddlers set off to explore the waterways at drop points along the way.

OHIO'S OWN CANAL

When Ohio saw the benefits the Erie Canal had for New York, that state wanted a similar infrastructure. It took seven years to hand dig, but in the end, the trip from Cleveland to Cincinnati took only eighty hours, a trip that had taken weeks before the canal.

One of the draws and wonderful aspects is the natural landmark's unique history. The O&E was dug mostly by hand from 1825 to 1832 and traversed by mules carrying boats filled with goods and passengers to Lake Erie, Portsmouth, and the Ohio River. This transformed trade in the region. Before the O&E was built, transporting agriculture outside of what remains today a farming region was challenging at best—construction of the O&E changed that.

From the trail, you can join trips on the Cuyahoga Valley Scenic Railroad, connecting one historical experience to another. From the Ira Trailhead in the southern area is a short ten-minute walk leading to Beaver Marsh, a popular place to stroll along paved pathways and boardwalk trails in a watchable wildlife area where beavers, otters, and waterbirds can be spotted regularly.

The towpath is generally busy during high season, and trail etiquette is an important thing to note. Look on the www.nps.gov/cuva official site for tips on how to be mindful on the path.

All year long, walkers, runners, hikers, bikers, and riders on horseback follow the Ohio and Erie Canalway, while paddlers set off to explore the waterways at drop points along the way.

Gateway Arch

MO

Your Must-See Guide

Since its conception by Finnish-American architect Eero Saarinen in the early 1960s and its completion in 1965, the monumental Gateway Arch has ferried millions of visitors to its top, where views of St. Louis sprawl out onto a lively city and the Mississippi River waterways. Its bases sink sixty feet beneath the cityscape, shielding it from earthquakes and high winds.

Tram tours to the top are coveted and last forty-five minutes to one hour. Booking advanced

reservations is a smart idea. Once you have your ticket, you can better plan your time. While waiting for your tram ride, explore interactive exhibits at the Museum at the Gateway Arch to learn more about the monument and stories of people who influenced activity in the region.

Beyond tram tours, touring Gateway Arch can be done along tree-lined paths, ponds on either side of the arch's base, and in places like the Explorers Garden on the monument's north side, where you can see plants that Native American communities in the area used for medicine and to make tribal crafts. Photographing the arch is best done during late afternoon and sunset—areas behind and in front of the Old Courthouse provide great views, and the courthouse is beautiful to photograph too.

Tour operators in the city provide cool ways to see the arch from the Mississippi River on day cruises and dinner cruises, where you can

A MONUMENT DEDICATED TO PEOPLE

The monument celebrates a pioneering history and has been dedicated to honor Native American cultures as a whole and particularly in this region. It also commemorates African American slaves Dred and Harriet Scott, as well as suffragette Virginia Minor, who fought for their freedoms at St. Louis's Old Courthouse.

view the magnificent structure, and on flightseeing tours that provide bird's-eye views of the area.

 Park Snapshot

This urban national park is home to the world's tallest arch—a six-hundred-and-thirty-foot steel monument towering over St. Louis, Missouri—and the largest human-made structure in the United States and the centerpiece of the park. It stretches from the historic Old Courthouse to the western banks of the Mississippi River. It's sometimes called the "Gateway to the West" (known as Jefferson National Expansion Memorial until the national park was established in 2018), and stories the path of explorers pushing west; namely, Lewis and Clark, who passed through the area with the aid and knowledge of their Shoshone guide Sacagawea on an expedition aimed at reaching the Pacific Ocean.

The main areas to visit are the arch itself, viewing it from either the base or on tram rides to the top, at the Museum at the Gateway Arch, and on the expansive grounds where local attractions, eateries, and accommodations are situated nearby.

• WHAT •

A steel monument arcing over St. Louis, Missouri, with a long history storying the journey of settlers in nineteenth-century America.

• WHERE •

In the center of the park, towering overhead.

• WHEN TO VISIT •

June through August is busy with summer vacationers. Late spring and fall bring many groups and class trips. Crowds thin out in November through March. Winter has mild weather and shorter lines, and is a great time to capture crowd-free pictures!

• HOW TO GET THERE •

In downtown St. Louis, park at public lots near Gateway Arch and the Old Courthouse. The west entrance is the park's main entry; the east entrance is accessible by Leonor K. Sullivan Boulevard, and boats arrive from the Mississippi River. The north entrance is on 1st and 2nd Streets.

AR

Bathhouse Row

Your Must-See Guide

When you step into the Fordyce Bathhouse Visitor Center and Museum, you are walking into a page of history. When you enter the Buckstaff Bathhouse just a few doors down—you can experience history for yourself with a traditional hydrotherapy treatment at one of only two bathhouses still operating on Bathhouse Row.

Fordyce was the most luxurious spa in its heyday, and today it is the best way for park visitors to wander through time. It opened in 1915 and was regarded as the most sophisticated and elegant of all

eight locations on Bathhouse Row, a most sought-after site for the elite who wanted to heal their bodies and minds in a so-called fountain of youth. The Victorian-style architecture was as striking street-side as it was within, with ornate marble doorways and fountains, stained glass windows glittering colorful patterns onto spacious sitting rooms, and a leather-clad gymnasium with speed bags and a pommel horse on the upper floors—all of which looks like a scene from a movie set. Fordyce welcomed American presidents, foreign dignitaries, celebrities, athletes, and Prohibition-era gangsters into its walls—preserving secrets with every droplet of steam.

Buckstaff is the only bathhouse still operating in its original structure, offering a traditional bathing experience akin to what was available more than one hundred years ago when it opened in 1912. A typical service might include a soak in high temperatures, hot towel treatments, full-body steam treatments,

GREAT HIKING AT HOT SPRINGS

The Sunset Trail hike is twelve miles all-in (and broken down into three smaller sections if you wish to hike only a portion of it). It is moderately strenuous depending on your physicality and leads through diverse forests to some of the highest points in the area.

sitz tub soaks, and cooldowns in freezing needle showers. If you want to be transported to another place, time, and full-body experience—Bathhouse Row is the place!

Park Snapshot

Hot Springs has several distinctive qualities that many crave in a park experience—cultural, historical, and natural—wrapped up in two distinct sections. The first is a small urban area where once-thriving bathhouses that enticed affluent visitors from the United States and Europe during the turn of the twentieth century are still standing. They were fueled by mineral-rich geothermal waters flowing from the western slope of Hot Springs Mountain. The second is Hot Springs Mountain itself, where you can explore dense hickory forests on foot and on scenic drives and hikes before resting your head at the national park campground.

Hot Springs is the oldest park unit, with its geothermal waters protected as a resource in 1832. Long before that, American Indians resourced novaculite for tools and weapons—it is said that arrowheads can still be found on Sugarloaf Mountain.

• WHAT •

Early twentieth-century bathhouses with stunning architectural features on a stroll-about street. The bathhouses originated because of the natural thermal waters in the area. In 1832, Hot Springs became the first national park unit to protect a natural resource.

• WHERE •

On Bathhouse Row located on Central Avenue, in the heart of the small, urban national park.

• WHEN TO VISIT •

March through November, when tours and services are regularly operating and when hiking weather is most favorable. September through May can offer a less-crowded experience. The few bathhouses still operating are open year-round.

• HOW TO GET THERE •

Head to the Fordyce Bathhouse Visitor Center to get a lay of the land and learn about the different locations in the national park area before heading onward to explore.

Lake Michigan Shoreline

IN

Your Must-See Guide

While the dunes are the heart of Indiana Dunes, the shoreline often steals the show. Fifteen miles of soft, sandy shoreline along southern Lake Michigan beckons park visitors for endless amounts of beachside fun. Whether it be relaxing by the water, flying kites or building sandcastles on the shore, or swimming in the sparkling waters—there is a reason this lake is sometimes referred to as "America's Third Coast."

There are nine beach areas along the vast stretch traveling through both national park and state parklands, coming together as one great destination for visitors. If you are interested in a quiet and serene experience, head to Kemil and its neighbor, Dunbar Beach. If you want to go where the action is, head to West Beach— where there are lifeguards on duty during summer months, covered picnic areas, and a concession stand. West Beach gives you direct access to the one-mile Dune Succession Trail, where wooden staircases enter the dune landscape and diverse plant and bird habitats (with two offshoot trails alongside it if you want to wander on a few more miles).

Mount Baldy Beach sits at the base of the largest living dune field in the park, perched one hundred and twenty-six feet above the water. You will need to join a ranger-led hike to explore it, and this is offered later in the day when colorful skies backdrop the shoreline, water, and the Chicago city skyline at the top

ADVENTURES IN INDIANA DUNES!

Ready for active adventures during your time at Indiana Dunes? Take the 3 Dune Challenge, hiking the three tallest dunes in the park. Participate in geocaching adventures to look for deliberately placed hidden treasures. Each year in September, the park's Outdoor Adventure Festival provides a fun way to end the summer season.

of the Mount Baldy Summit Trail—a phenomenal scene to capture at sunset.

 Park Snapshot

This park is cradled by dynamic sand dunes formed by Ice Age–era glaciers, rooted with rugged vegetation that can be so dense it often hides the dunes from view. It is one of the most biodiverse parks in the system, where grasslands, swamps, and wetlands provide habitat to some of the most peculiar and interesting plants you've ever seen. The spongy landscape is an important feeding and resting ground for migratory birds and is so healthy that more than three hundred and fifty species have been documented here. Just under fifty miles of established trails lead through every kind of awesome environment imaginable. From bogs to beaches, forests to marshes—the more you explore, the more variety you will uncover in an amazingly rich natural world. Historical sites like the Bailly Homestead and Chellberg Farm and the Century of Progress Homes showcase different eras of architecture offering plenty of cool photo ops along the way.

• WHAT •

Fifteen miles of sandy coastline on the shores of Lake Michigan, with grassy dunes and rugged ecosystems stretching inland.

• WHERE •

The northern edge of the park, sharing a boundary with the adjacent state park, on the southern shores of Lake Michigan.

• WHEN TO VISIT •

Late May through September, when weather is warmest and allows for more water-based and beachfront activities.

• HOW TO GET THERE •

There are several access roads to the national park beach areas, and most have free parking lots either right next to them or a short walk away. If entering from the west side, head to the Paul H. Douglas Center for Environmental Education for beach access information; if entering from the east, stop at the Dorothy Buell Memorial Visitor Center.

Boat Ride to the Rock Harbor Lighthouse

MI

Your Must-See Guide

Encircled by cobalt-blue waters and rocky rugged coastline, you are in for both stunning scenery and excitement while exploring the perimeter of Isle Royale—a can't-miss experience when visiting the national park.

One of the most popular day trips is to the Edisen Fishery and Rock Harbor Lighthouse, which you can visit aboard a concessionaire-operated boat with an experienced ship captain at the helm. While onboard the *MV Sandy* sea vessel on a half-day tour, you will learn

BE PREPARED TO UNPLUG

Because of its remote location, Isle Royale has no communications signals, so plan to fully unplug and enjoy your surroundings (and some of the starriest night skies in the lower forty-eight states). Limited access can mean slightly higher prices in Rock Harbor, the only place to buy simple goods on the island.

about the island national park and the glacier-formed waterways that surround it—which behave much more like an ocean than they do a freshwater lake.

Upon landing and after a short greeting from the Park Service, there are three main areas to explore: the Rock Harbor Lighthouse, a small museum that sits beside it, and the historic Edisen Fishery. The lighthouse is the oldest on the island, built in 1855 and serving as a reliable guide to help mariners navigate the rocky coastlines. Although it is no longer illuminated, it still draws visitors with its picturesque beauty. Sitting at its side is a museum where you can wander the grounds of keepers from long ago while learning about the lighthouse's history through maritime exhibits and ranger-led talks. Less than half a mile away on a short trail is the old Edisen Fishery and the historic Bangsund Cabin, which serves as the hub of the longest continuously running predator/prey study in the world, examining the relationship between the wolves and moose of the north woods.

Park Snapshot

On the northeast side of Lake Superior, the largest of the Great Lakes, rises a pristine forested archipelago from its cool waters. Isle Royale is one of the least visited and most revisited national parks, made up of 95 percent untapped wilderness.

There are only two established areas. Windigo in the south is a starting point for backpackers and hikers planning to make their way up the island on foot across forty-five miles and for paddlers taking on portaging adventures riding shorelines and lakes before carrying their watercraft to new drop points. On the north end of the island is Rock Harbor, offering the only services on Isle Royale and several day trips to visitors.

The island brims with vibrant life after long winters when the park is closed. Wildflowers color hardwood forests and shorelines, moose slurp up aquatic grasses in inland lakes, and the haunting call of the loon echoes across the northern waters.

• WHAT •

The oldest and most visited lighthouse on Isle Royale, with an adjoining museum that once served as the keeper's house.

• WHERE •

In the northeast area of the park, at the southwest entrance to Rock Harbor on the edge of the Saginaw Peninsula.

• WHEN TO VISIT •

Early June to early September, when *MV Sandy* ship tours are operating along the coastlines. Isle Royale is entirely closed to visitors from October through May.

• HOW TO GET THERE •

Isle Royale is accessible only by chartered or privately operated sea vessel or by floatplane with routes leading directly to Rock Harbor. Once you are on land, head to the concessionaire-operated Rock Harbor Lodge office to obtain schedule information and tickets for the boat tour.

The South Unit

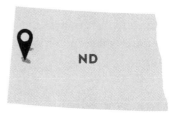

ND

Your Must-See Guide

When entering the South Unit of Theodore Roosevelt National Park, all signs seem to point first to the Painted Canyon Overlook, just a stone's throw away from the Painted Canyon Visitor Center. Along a long paved pathway hugging the rim, panoramic views of magnificent scenery pan out in every direction, offering a taste of the wild Dakota region.

From the overlook, many head out along the one-mile Painted Canyon Nature Trail or along the four-mile out-and-back Painted Canyon Trail, both experiences that allow you to get to know the countryside that inspired Theodore Roosevelt's conservation of the area.

After a journey on foot, relax in your vehicle along the scenic loop drive that winds thirty-six miles through painted sandstone, where fossils hide beneath forested areas that sprout from the hillsides. It is as beautiful as it is exhilarating, as throngs of big-game wildlife can quite literally stop you in your tracks. Minding the twenty-five-mile-per-hour speed limit is essential and will serve you well in an area where herds of American bison, elk, longhorn steer, and other large and small mammals emerge from dense vegetation at all times of the day and night. In the surrounding areas are wild horses grazing in fields farther from the road—they are the only wild horses in the flagship national parks. Theodore Roosevelt's Maltese Cross Cabin is a cool historical stop you can make to see where he first lived in the park before building Elkhorn Ranch

A TOWN FOR THE "DOGS"

Try to see the large prairie dog town along the Scenic Loop Drive near the Old East Entrance Trail. It is worth pulling your car over and spending a few minutes watching the intriguing little creatures interact. Prairie dogs will "bark" at you if you get too close to their burrows.

(which makes up the West Unit) and where he lived during most of his time there.

 Park Snapshot

The Dakotas have drawn seekers of frontier lands for centuries, where rugged horse trails met by unspoiled lands held the promise of a new way of life focused on the natural world. That was the dream of Theodore Roosevelt, and it is one that remains for national park enthusiasts dedicated to understanding North America's purest natural environments.

The park is composed of three areas. The North Unit is quiet and rugged, with excellent camping and backcountry hikes as well as unusual formations such as the curious Cannonball Concretions. The South Unit is a sanctuary for wildlife, historical landmarks, and incredible landscapes that could easily capture your attention for days on end. The West Unit is where you can walk in Theodore Roosevelt's footsteps at the remains of his former home at Elkhorn Ranch for a long afternoon of exploring, learning, and reflecting. All are bound by the Little Missouri River, the lifeblood of the region.

• WHAT •

The easiest-to-get-to and most popular section of the national park, with a scenic drive, colorful landscapes, and watchable wildlife.

• WHERE •

In the South Unit of the national park, near the town of Medora, North Dakota.

• WHEN TO VISIT •

From May through October, when the weather is most pleasant and most predictable. Visitor center hours vary in each of the three units throughout the year. Winter brings snow, ice, and closures, so check in advance for off-season accessibility.

• HOW TO GET THERE •

There are two visitor centers in the south area of the park—the Painted Canyon Visitor Center and the South Unit Visitor Center located in the town of Medora. Both are great places to kick off your journey.

Elkhorn Ranch

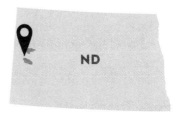

ND

Your Must-See Guide

Elkhorn Ranch is where President Theodore Roosevelt, known as the "conservationist president," lived for nearly thirteen years. It is the least visited area of the park, has no services or landmarks apart from the ranch area, and can be hard to find since so few visitors go there. All of that makes it more exciting!

Roosevelt came to the Dakota Territory after the passing of his mother and wife, both of which tragically occurred on the same day. He built the Maltese Cross Cabin in the South Unit (still there today and worthy of a stop), then started

OFF THE GRID

With no services, facilities, or paved roadways and few signs leading to an area with no cellular service or Wi-Fi—you will find yourself in true remote Dakota Territory! That is part of the allure. When Roosevelt lived here, the only way to his ranch was on horseback.

building Elkhorn Ranch, which took a year to complete. On the grounds were stables, cattle grounds, a chicken coop, and a blacksmith. All that remains today are remnants of the foundational structure beneath towering cottonwood trees where elk roam peacefully across the landscape as they did when Roosevelt was there.

There is seemingly little to see there—which might make naming it a must-see site seem odd—but it is of extreme historical significance, and if you tap in to your imagination, you'll understand why it's earning a spot on this list. The area is preserved as a historic site for those who want to walk in Roosevelt's footsteps and see the place that ultimately turned him into one of the greatest champions of conservation in the history of the United States. The structure was thirty feet by sixty feet, containing eight rooms protected by seven-foot-high walls with a porch overlooking the Little Missouri River.

The area is preserved as a historic site for those who want to walk in Roosevelt's footsteps and see the place that ultimately turned him into one of the greatest champions of conservation in the history of the United States.

• WHAT •

The land where Theodore Roosevelt lived during much of his time there, where pieces of the structural foundation remain.

• WHERE •

The West Unit of the national park, between the North and South Units.

• WHEN TO VISIT •

May through October during high season and when road conditions are best to travel there.

• HOW TO GET THERE •

From either the North or South Unit, take I-94 to Exit 23 before traveling thirty-five miles on rugged road (four-wheel drive is ideal for the last three miles, depending on conditions). It can be a challenge to find, as it's not well marked, and you'll travel through private land to get there. Your best bet is to stop at a park visitor center and ask for detailed directions before heading out.

Kettle Falls

MN

Your Must-See Guide

Water-based exploration is so great at Voyageurs that many never venture off the lakes and onto dry land beyond shoreside camping spots. When they do, however, a long and colorful past of the region unfolds at a handful of historical areas such as at Kettle Falls—a central point of travel hundreds of years ago and a conduit through the northern border and wilderness.

Native communities hunted and fished at the falls, voyageurs crossed through on canoes transporting furs and other valuable items for trade, and prospectors used it as a waypoint en route to mines at Rainy Lake where gold was sourced from ancient quartz rock. Those who built the area patronized the Kettle Falls Hotel during the logging era before it transitioned into a coveted tourist spot. This background outlines just a sampling of stories you will hear during your time at Kettle Falls—and you're certain to learn many more during ranger-led activities, such as how the hotel was once advertised as a sanctuary for hay-fever victims cured by pine-cleansed air that we are all free to experience today.

Whether you are visiting on a day trip or staying overnight at the Kettle Falls Hotel, you will inevitably stop at the dams located not far from the national park's only accommodations, overlooking points of interest with views of Canada in the distance. Back at the hotel, wander the forested grounds before stepping

WHAT IS A VOYAGEUR?

Voyageurs are French-Canadian fur traders who traveled the interconnected waterways of the Great Lakes by canoe into interior country, creating trade routes with Native Americans in the eighteenth and nineteenth centuries. Voyageurs sought navigation guidance and goods such as valuable beaver hats while offering food, clothing, medicine, and information in return.

inside to have a meal, take a drink in the famed slope-floored bar, and relax on the wraparound veranda.

Park Snapshot

Voyageurs National Park is all about water, and the best way to truly explore it is by boat. With more than two hundred thousand acres of wilderness and nine hundred islands resting on freshwater highways that course through Minnesota's north woods on the Canadian border, there is plenty of land and water to explore. Selecting a jumping-off point is the first step, and the National Park Service has marked thirteen prime visitor destinations to help ease navigation. You can learn about these on the official park website for Voyageurs: www.nps.gov/voya.

Once you've decided where to base your adventure, there are endless activities to enjoy all year long. Whether it be houseboating, camping, fishing, or paddling the water world the way it was traveled centuries ago; exploring lakes, streams, and wetlands that hug the base of some of the oldest and most colorful rocks on Earth; or hiking boreal and northern hardwood forests—epic adventures await!

• WHAT •

The main historic travel route through the area and one of the best places to experience the natural and cultural history of the park.

• WHERE •

At the eastern edge of the Kabetogama Peninsula, where Rainy Lake and Namakan Lake intersect, in the northeast area of the park.

• WHEN TO VISIT •

Voyageurs is open year-round. Kettle Falls is most popular June through August when access onto the water is widely available. Late September and October treat visitors with wonderful displays of colorful fall foliage.

• HOW TO GET THERE •

Kettle Falls is accessible only by boat or floatplane, either privately or commercially operated or by approved concessionaires. You can get to Kettle Falls from four park visitor centers: Ash River, Brule Narrows, Kabetogama Lake, or Rainy Lake.

Wind Cave

SD

Your Must-See Guide

To native Lakota Indians in South Dakota, the whistling wind gusting from the only known natural cave entrance at Wind Cave is a sacred reflection of the underworld emerging into the earthly landscape. To geologists, that event is the phenomenon of atmospheric pressure shifting between above- and belowground temperatures. The cave became a curiosity to prospectors during the Gold Rush era, when new people were drawn to the area. When mining subsided, travel into

MAXIMIZE YOUR TIME IN SOUTH DAKOTA

If you can extend your time in the area and want to knock a bunch of National Park Service sites off your list while seeing several of South Dakota's most fascinating places, pair your trip with ones to Badlands National Park, Jewel Cave National Monument, Mount Rushmore, and Custer State Park.

the mysterious underground caverns welcomed even more people.

Today's visitors are struck by how spacious the cave is and by unexpected breezes formed by wind systems that are unusual to experience inside a subterranean environment. The fascination continues with stalactites (hanging from the ceiling); stalagmites (rising from the ground); flowstone that looks like earthly waves; chunky popcorn; draped curtain formations—and a favorite to many: cave bacon, which looks exactly like a piece of bacon in color and texture. Wind Cave also protects the world's largest concentration of rare boxwork formations made of calcite, which looks a bit like gothic honeycomb stretched across the ceiling. Rangers will enthusiastically detail this feature during short trips on the Garden of Eden Tour and on longer excursions on the full-day Fairgrounds Tour. What makes the guided trips at Wind Cave even cooler is knowing that you are traveling in with knowledgeable rangers who are also some of the most experienced cavers out there, some of whom participate in cave rescue operations all across the world.

Park Snapshot

Wind Cave National Park is a dream for those who love variety in a national park experience, with underground cave adventures and an aboveground environment that is perfect for activities such as biking, hiking, backpacking, camping, wildlife watching, and photography.

The cave itself is a subject of great interest to cavers and scientific researchers alike who want to explore and understand one of the world's oldest caves and all that comes with it—including unusual cave formations (scientifically referred to as "speleothems") such as the planet's finest sample of boxwork that decorates the ceilings of underground passageways.

On the prairie landscape, wildlife roams peacefully across grasslands and in forested areas. The Beaver Creek area of the park scarcely sees visitors and is home to grasslands, forests, and wetlands where wildlife and vegetation are in their purest form.

• WHAT •

Wind Cave was the first national park established to protect a cave system and is one of the oldest, largest, and most complex subterranean chambers on Earth.

• WHERE •

On the southwest side of the national park.

• WHEN TO VISIT •

May through September is high season and is when the most ranger-led tours operate. Shoulder seasons are recommended, as July and August can bring soaring temperatures that make aboveground hiking less comfortable—and the trails in the area are not to be missed.

• HOW TO GET THERE •

There are three entrances to the park on the north, south, and east sides. Once there, head to the Wind Cave Visitor Center, where an elevator will bring you into the cave.

Aboveground Animal Viewing

SD

Your Must-See Guide

While a visit to Wind Cave couldn't be complete without a trip underground to explore the caverns, exploring aboveground is a must while in this national park. Blanketing the landscape is mixed grassland prairie as well as aspen and pine forests that are havens to animal and birdlife populations. The area's unique weather patterns often turn up spectacular skies filled with colorful sunsets, rainbows, and cloud formations that provide a picturesque backdrop to animals

DO NOT FEED THE ANIMALS

Feeding the wildlife in any national park is illegal for several reasons. Animals who get used to feeding from human hands become less timid of humans and can become food-aggressive. Human food may also make the animals sick or worse. Lastly, the animals could be carrying diseases that could put you in danger if you are in close contact.

including American bison, elk, deer, and coyote, and the fastest animal in North America: the pronghorn. Day after day, animals saunter across rolling hills, where prairie dog communities alert other "towns" of the presence of larger predators through audible song. Wandering the skies are migrating birds such as the black-backed woodpecker—a coveted sighting for birders in North America. If you are lucky, you might see the only animal in the area on the Critically Endangered species list, the black-footed ferret (typically seen after dark).

The main paved park road has plenty of pull-offs where you can stop to view wildlife from a safe distance, with the fabled South Dakota Black Hills lying across the horizon. There are other rugged areas in the north and east areas of the park where wildlife sightings will be more common in the more secluded environment. However you plan your wildlife viewing excursion, know that there are nearly thirty thousand acres of protected sanctuary to explore from the comfort of your vehicle, making it nearly impossible to travel without seeing cool wildlife along the way!

The main paved park road has plenty of pull-offs where you can stop to view wildlife from a safe distance, with the fabled South Dakota Black Hills lying across the horizon.

CHAPTER 5

Northeast Region

Cadillac Mountain

ME

Your Must-See Guide

The first visible rays of sunrise in the United States shine at 1,530 feet above sea level at the top of Cadillac Mountain each morning from October through March; the rest of the year, other high points on the Eastern Seaboard take that crown. Whenever you visit, panoramic views of a spectacular glaciated coastal landscape await when the clouds part atop Cadillac Mountain, with views over the Gulf of Maine, Frenchman Bay, the Schoodic Peninsula, and Bar Harbor.

Cadillac Mountain is the highest of twenty mountains on Mount Desert Island, which formed over the course of millions of years of volcanic and tectonic activity as the continents shifted—a remarkable thing to consider given that today, you can take a leisurely drive up Cadillac Summit Road to catch views of it all. The road leads to a parking area at the top where you can set up with a picnic and a camera, or simply grab a seat to take in breathtaking views that are especially colorful at sunrise and sunset.

There are other adventurous ways to reach the top of the mountain while breaking a sweat along the way. Along the over-seven-mile round-trip Cadillac South Ridge Trail, you can hike, bike, or ride on horseback along varying terrain with epic views along the way. The over-four-mile Cadillac North Ridge Trail provides a taste of the terrain on a steep trail line that leads to a resting area surrounded by sublime beauty. Other trails to the top include the Gorge Path, North Ridge, and West Face Trail.

WHAT'S IN A NAME?

Until the 1900s, Cadillac Mountain was known as Green Mountain. Its name was changed to honor Antoine Laumet de la Mothe, sieur de Cadillac, a French explorer who laid claim to Mount Desert Island in the late 1680s.

Park Snapshot

Acadia was the first national park established east of the Mississippi River and was created the same year as the National Park Service in 1916. Local residents fought for the land to remain wild, buying it up and donating it to the federal government to ensure preservation.

The park has a distinct northeastern style, and adventure abounds—whether it be biking across stone carriage roads and bridges, photographing bulbous stones shaped by the Atlantic Ocean on Boulder Beach, or wandering the carved-out shoreline on the Ocean Path, you'll never have a dull moment in Acadia.

The main park area sits on Mount Desert Island, where trails, scenic drives, and other natural landmarks dot the landscape before giving way to the sea. The Schoodic Peninsula section is an outlier in terms of both location and visitation and is a favorite area for locals and wildlife alike who prefer fewer crowds and wilder scenery.

• WHAT •

The highest point on the North Atlantic seacoast and site of the first glimpse of sunrise in the United States for half of the year.

• WHERE •

In the southeast section of the main area of protected parkland located on Mount Desert Island.

• WHEN TO VISIT •

May through October (fall foliage usually pops from late September through mid-October). Acadia is open all year round but is still a seasonal park. Most facilities are either closed or operate during off-season hours from mid-October through late May.

• HOW TO GET THERE •

Access to Cadillac Summit Road is located at either the start or end of Acadia's Park Loop Road and winds three and a half miles up a paved roadway to the summit to the parking area.

Jordan Pond and Jordan Pond House

ME

Your Must-See Guide

From the glacier-carved lake setting to a summertime tradition of gathering for tea, Jordan Pond provides memorable moments in Acadia that visitors seek year after year—where recreation converges with conversation! There are two popular areas to explore here: Jordan Pond, a glass-surface lake with incredible clarity surrounded by mountains and forests, and the Jordan Pond House, the only full-service restaurant in the park.

Along the almost-three-and-a-half-mile Jordan Pond Path, you can immerse yourself in peaceful nature that is classic Acadia on an even dirt pathway surrounding the lake. Views of South Bubble and North Bubble mountains (collectively called "The Bubbles") greet you from the start of the trailhead, reflecting perfectly against the calm and clear waters that make this scene so beautiful (and really fun to photograph!). This is not a recreational lake—boating, swimming, fishing, and wading are not permitted—allowing it to remain immaculately pure and to continue serving as a water source for the area.

The Island Explorer shuttle bus has pickup and drop-off service all summer long at the nearby Jordan Pond House, which is just a short stroll away from the lake's trailhead. The Jordan Pond House is a destination all its own, welcoming visitors to taste the regional history with the service of tea, popovers, and berry jam that have delighted visitors there since the 1890s. It is a popular destination to conclude hikes, bike rides, and horseback rides.

CAPTURE PHOTOS OF THE BASS HARBOR HEAD LIGHT!

The Bass Harbor Head Light is an incredible scene to both see and photograph—statuesquely perched fifty-six feet above the rocky Atlantic shoreline where its red blinking light calls out to the sea at night. Its best viewpoint is just a short walk with a few stairs from the parking area.

The Jordan Pond House is a destination all its own, welcoming visitors to taste the regional history with the service of tea, popovers, and berry jam that have delighted visitors there since the 1890s.

A pristine inland lake surrounded by mountains and a historic stop for an afternoon tea in traditional fashion.

In the southeast area of Mount Desert Island, the most frequented area of the park.

June to early September has the warm weather and skies clear of intense fog that coastal Maine is known for. It is also the busiest time of year. April and May are lovely times to explore during shoulder season, though many services may still be closed. September and October offer cooler temperatures and are prime times for fall foliage.

Drive the just under three miles from the Hulls Cove Visitor Center and continue along Park Loop Road following signs for Jordan Pond.

Long Point Trail

WV

Your Must-See Guide

A trip to this national park couldn't be complete without viewing its most famous feature: the New River Gorge Bridge—the longest steel span in the Western Hemisphere and the third highest in the United States, with massive vertical and arced steel beams anchoring it to the ground. The bridge is as fashionable as it is functional, greatly reducing travel time from one side of the gorge to the other. At the end of Long Point Trail, you'll have direct views of the bridge while perched upon a rocky outcrop where a panoramic landscape of tree-covered

gorge stretches out in all directions. The just-over-one-and-a-half-mile out-and-back trail is a fun, short route for hikers, bikers, and sightseers. You will pass through field then forest in a peaceful shaded setting that is relatively easy (depending on your level of physical fitness) with one steep area just before you hit the Long Point Overlook. Bring your camera, a picnic, and your favorite people and stay awhile, though you should note that the viewpoint is popular and therefore usually congested during busy day-hiking hours and at sunset, but you can usually find a spot if you head out a little early. Catching the scene at sunrise can be beautiful if the clouds part to reveal the first rays of daylight sun cast upon the forested gorge. If you are not a fan of exposure, you may struggle at the main viewpoint, but have no fear—there are incredible views standing a clear distance from the edge.

CHECK FOR CLOSURES

The steep terrain of the gorge adds to its beauty, but it also makes it prone to slides and washouts. This in turn can close or temporarily shut down the roads and trails in the park. Be sure to check the park's website before heading there for any updated information on closures.

Park Snapshot

West Virginia is called the "Mountain State," and from any point in the park you will see wooded slopes cascading one thousand feet into one of the oldest rivers in North America: the New River (casually called "the New"), which flows northwesterly rather than southward like most rivers on the continent.

Such an environment makes adventure opportunities as plentiful as they are easy to find, whether hiking along one hundred miles of established trails, climbing rock faces, or paddling the New on calm waters leading to Class 4+ rapids. Modern infrastructure as well as historical structures from the booming coal mining era lie in untamed wilderness and preserve areas, where local residents (and those with permits) can hunt and fish in the protected area the way they always have. If you are after a more relaxed adventure, there are waterfalls, viewpoints, and easy nature trails that allow enjoyment of this incredible piece of North America.

• WHAT •

An easy day hike along a nature trail to one of the clearest views of the New River Gorge Bridge.

• WHERE •

In the north section of the park, near the Canyon Rim Visitor Center.

• WHEN TO VISIT •

April through October serves up the best weather in New River Gorge in terms of temperatures and conditions. October has gorgeous fall foliage as well as the annual Bridge Day fall park festival.

• HOW TO GET THERE •

Access to Long Point Trail starts in the town of Fayetteville, traveling WV 16 to Gatewood Road (County Road 9) to Newton Road, located just under two miles from the trailhead. You can also park at the trailheads for Kaymoor Miners Trail and Butcher Branch Trail.

Sandstone Falls

WV

Your Must-See Guide

Love waterfalls? If so, you cannot miss the scene at Sandstone Falls. This site is a bit of a drive from more commonly visited northern areas of the park, and it is worth every mile of road traveled once you reach the fifteen-hundred-foot-wide cascading falls that stretch across the New River, cutting through smoothed boulders of layered ancient river rock. Both wild and serene, this area marks a transition point between the New River and its confluence with the Gauley River, which forms the larger Kanawha River.

CATCH BRIDGE DAY IN OCTOBER!

Bridge Day is celebrated annually on the third Sunday of October, the only day of the year the bridge is closed to cars and open to foot traffic. With incredible views, vendors, and the annual BASE jump into the gorge, this is a festive and fun time to be in the park.

The Sandstone Falls day-use area provides easy walking across flat boardwalk and bridge networks that channel through diverse vegetation, including the unique botanical ecosystem of the Appalachian Riverside Flatrock Community. From there, you are mere steps away from gorgeous views of the main falls. At the edge of the river, you can venture onward on unmarked trails to blaze your own path while rock hopping across scrambles to stunning close-up views that are fun to see and photograph from all angles. As it is with all natural areas near powerful waterways, be sure to explore carefully and mind your step.

As you drive in or out from the parking area, try to take some time to stop along the scenic eight-mile River Road to check out overlooks and view the river from a different vantage point. There are plenty of cultural sites to check out in neighboring towns as well, such as the historic district and the railroad museum in the small town of Hinton.

At the edge of the river, you can venture onward on unmarked trails to blaze your own path while rock hopping across scrambles to stunning close-up views that are fun to see and photograph from all angles.

The largest waterfall on the New River with a wide span surrounded by rocky outcrops and established trails.

In the south section of the national park.

April through October has the warmest weather and is when water flow is highest, making the falls even more spectacular. This area is open year-round.

Travel Route 20 from I-64 to the small town of Sandstone and ten miles to the town of Hinton, which connects to the park's only scenic drive along River Road for eight miles. You can also catch a bird's-eye view of the falls from six hundred feet above them at the Sandstone Falls Overlook, located just under three miles south on WV 20 from the Sandstone Visitor Center.

Skyline Drive

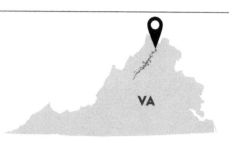

VA

Your Must-See Guide

No visit to Shenandoah could be fully realized without traveling Skyline Drive. The historic scenic roadway is the main vein of the park, and it is the only public road found there. With every mile marker, there are new wonders to explore as you travel through one hundred and five miles of Virginia's Blue Ridge Mountains. Skyline Drive is a gateway to popular trailheads, more than seventy-five scenic viewpoints that overlook the Shenandoah Valley, and notable

locations that describe the region where the country was founded.

A great day on Skyline Drive is made up of variety. You can plan on exploring by car virtually all day long and breaking up your time by heading out on hikes into hidden forests that lead to rocky outcrops and cascading waterfalls where animals and birds are with you every step of the way—whether you know it or not! As the day turns to night, many prepare to catch last light while lounging on grassy areas with a picnic while the sun falls behind the horizon.

Bird lovers are in heaven as woodpeckers, barn owls, red-tailed hawks, and chickadees seem to glide alongside you for the length of your journey. In the summer, the road is lively—with motorcyclists, road bikers, and auto-tourists enjoying the warm mid-Atlantic summer air. Fall is one of the best times to visit, when yellow canopies of dancing leaves are matched identically in color to the yellow stripes that cut through the cement roadway.

TWO DIFFERENT ROADS

People often mistakenly think that Skyline Drive is the same road as the Blue Ridge Parkway. Skyline Drive runs through Shenandoah National Park, while the Blue Ridge Parkway does not actually enter the park's grounds. The southern entrance to Shenandoah National Park is also the northern terminus of the Blue Ridge Parkway, which is one of the factors that leads to confusion.

Park Snapshot

Shenandoah's proximity to the suburbs of northern Virginia and the Washington, DC, metro area makes it a favorite local spot for easy day trips into nature, while beckoning travelers from around the world at the same time. Road-trippers delight in the famed Skyline Drive, which is without a doubt one of the most fun-to-drive roadways in North America. In this park, you never know what a day might bring. Heading off on foot, you could come across any number of finds, such as historical relics; a run-in with day hikers traveling through on the Appalachian Trail; or wildlife—some elusive, like black bear, coyote, and fox; others more commonly seen, like deer, racoons, and wild turkeys. Hiking is a major draw with trails of varying lengths and difficulty. Some lead along nature paths, and others to sky-high vantage points where you can take in panoramic views that reveal a painted landscape.

• WHAT •

A paved scenic byway traveling the crest of the fabled Blue Ridge Mountains.

• WHERE •

The main vein cutting through the heart of the national park, beginning in Front Royal on the north end of the Shenandoah Valley, winding to Waynesboro to meet the Blue Ridge Parkway in the south.

• WHEN TO VISIT •

April through October, when most facilities are open. Portions of Skyline Drive are closed during inclement weather. September and October are optimal viewing times for peak fall foliage.

• HOW TO GET THERE •

There are four access points to Skyline Drive: Front Royal Entrance Station (Front Royal, Virginia), Thornton Gap Entrance Station (near Luray, Virginia), Swift Run Gap Entrance Station (near Elkton, Virginia), and Rockfish Gap Entrance Station (the northern entrance to the Blue Ridge Parkway).

Old Rag

VA

Your Must-See Guide

Old Rag is a bucket list hike in the mid-Atlantic region. There are two main routes leading to the top of Old Rag Mountain, which stands at 3,284 feet. At this elevation, you will stand in the clouds with 360-degree views overlooking the Shenandoah Valley.

The just-over-nine-mile Old Rag Circuit is the most popular route to the summit and is where you will find huge rock scrambles, which, to many people, are what make the hike so awesome. The lollipop trail (a trail with a loop at the end of an out-and-back start/finish) wanders through shady forested areas and gains elevation along switchbacks before hitting a series of complex scrambles as you near the top. The giant granite boulders require large upward and downward steps and a reasonable amount of upper-body strength (although it is not a technical climb). You are highly unlikely to find solitude on this route, and congestion can add quite a bit of time.

Hiking to the summit starting from Berry Hollow forgoes the scrambles but is strenuous because of the rapid elevation gain across the almost five and a half miles. This route is a little less crowded than the Circuit Trail and offers a lot of the same great nature.

If you aren't interested in hiking to the top of Old Rag but still want to experience the mountain, the Nicholson Hollow Trail follows eight miles round trip but with only 1,240 elevation gain. The Robertson Mountain Trail is almost eight miles round trip following fire roads. Both are great if you have a pet in tow.

KNOW YOUR LIMITS AND PREPARE

The two summit routes to the top of Old Rag are incredible and are both epic physical challenges, so assess your ability level before you take on either one. Pack lightly and bring plenty of water and a map either downloaded on your phone or printed and in your pocket.

The just-over-nine-mile Old Rag Circuit is the most popular route to the summit and is where you will find huge rock scrambles, which, to many people, are what make the hike so awesome.

Pacific West Region

Santa Cruz Island

CA

Your Must-See Guide

Santa Cruz is California's largest island and is a beloved gem in the Channel Islands, marrying seagoing fun in protected ocean waters with a world of natural island beauty onshore.

It is home to one of the largest and deepest sea caves in the world, the Painted Cave, where you can set off on guided paddle adventures through rock archways on the northern coastline. The waters lining the caves protect nutrient-rich kelp habitats, where seals and sea lions

ACTIVE RESEARCH ON SANTA CRUZ

The National Park Service manages 24 percent of Santa Cruz Island, and the remainder is managed by the Nature Conservancy. Some of their joint efforts include protection and rehabilitation of historical and cultural sites, non-native plant and animal removal, recovery of island foxes, reintroduction of bald eagles, and wetland restoration.

can be seen popping their heads to the surface near your kayak before darting onward.

Hiking is the most popular activity on the island. There are relatively easy routes on maintained trails in the Scorpion Valley area, while the mountainous Montañon section has more challenging trails across rugged terrain. Along the four-and-a-half-mile Scorpion Canyon Loop Trail, you can witness the breadth of the island as you wander its peaks and valleys. This is where you may see the island scrub jay and Santa Cruz Island foxes (two species living only on Santa Cruz), beautiful flora, and breathtaking views of the California coastline. The almost-eight-mile Smugglers Cove Trail leads to tide pools at the halfway point where you can look for sea stars, urchins, and anemones on the tidal shoreline.

Trips to Santa Cruz start at Scorpion Cove, where the visitor center will help you get oriented straightaway. If you are staying overnight at the island's only established campground, you will find it not far away in two areas, a lower loop and an upper loop, in Scorpion Canyon.

 Park Snapshot

Off the coast of bustling Southern California is an island chain protecting a wild natural ecosystem on five islands that make up Channel Islands National Park: Anacapa, Santa Cruz, Santa Rosa, San Miguel, and Santa Barbara Islands. The marine sanctuary surrounding them protects a thriving network of aquatic plants and animals encircling rocky coastlines, island sea caves shaped by strong oceanic trade winds and currents, and expansive beaches.

The islands' geology dates back as far as one hundred million years. Human history is younger but still ancient with discovered artifacts dating back nearly thirteen thousand years—showcasing a timeline of the native Chumash, European settlers, explorers, ranchers, researchers, and, of course, national park visitors!

Enormous populations of bird species and unique animals live there, among panoramic views of the Pacific capped off with colorful California sunrises and sunsets.

• WHAT •

The largest and most popular of the five Channel Islands in the national park, with trails, camping, and paddling opportunities as well as unique wildlife and birdlife.

• WHERE •

On the east side of the island managed by the National Park Service.

• WHEN TO VISIT •

June through September is the most popular time, when the water is warmest and visibility is best, reaching close to one hundred feet beneath the ocean's surface. Trips to Santa Cruz operate year-round on a five-to-seven-day-a-week schedule.

• HOW TO GET THERE •

Take a one-hour (each way), twenty-five-mile boat ride from Ventura Harbor near Santa Barbara to Santa Cruz with Island Packers Cruises, the national park's only concessionaire, which operates trips to Santa Cruz and the other Channel Islands.

Crater Lake Lodge

OR

Your Must-See Guide

This must-see stop is a two-for-one with a visit to one of the most historic national park lodges of them all with one of the best views there is of what is hands down the most spectacular feature of the park: majestic Crater Lake!

Sitting on the patio, you can relax with your loved ones while gazing onto a lake known for its perfect reflection—resulting from its depth, absence of sediment, and seemingly hidden streams that flow out to the sea. In just that one moment, you'll want to raise a cup of cocoa or a craft cocktail (possible thanks to patio service from the lodge restaurant) for a celebratory toast of all you are seeing.

To get to that view, you will need to enter the lobby, where you are sure to be awed by massive native evergreen trees rising from the floor and onward through the ceiling. From there, you will enter the Great Hall with a centerpiece stone fireplace crackling coziness into the parlor where visitors play games, read books, and share in conversation. Opposite the fireplace is the back deck, where wood rocking chairs line up side by side to face directly onto the 7,700-year-old collapsed volcano turned caldera—quiet and still and reflecting the forested wilderness that surrounds it.

The Crater Lake Lodge is the quintessence of what was envisioned by early park champions like Stephen Mather, John Muir, and President Theodore Roosevelt—all of whom have peered across the same view.

PLAN AHEAD FOR WEATHER

There are seasonal road closures of the North Entrance and Rim Drive, sometimes making road travel difficult and even impossible due to snowy conditions resulting from high altitude (6,178 feet) and impeding access to wonderful parts of the park.

Park Snapshot

You know a place is special when you can hear audible gasps by onlookers, and that is likely what you will witness when standing before Crater Lake. Native Klamath of the region believed it to be so profoundly spiritual that only the wise could see it.

Crater Lake is the deepest lake in the United States, with 4.6 trillion gallons of water and impossibly blue reflective waters. Some make it a point to jump in (designated areas only), while others simply enjoy the scenery by car or bicycle along the paved thirty-three-mile Rim Drive that skirts the caldera. There are ninety miles of established hiking trails around the lake that are popular in both summer and winter, when trails are explored on snow machines, skis, and on foot. To see the lake from a different vantage point and enjoy warm summer days, head out on a boat tour to Wizard Island!

• WHAT •

A historic national park lodge with magnificent views of Crater Lake.

• WHERE •

Just south of Crater Lake, in the central area of the park.

• WHEN TO VISIT •

The lodge is open May through October; peak season for visitation to the park is late June through early October, when roads are most likely to be free of snow, making road transit possible.

• HOW TO GET THERE •

Most travel to Crater Lake National Park by car. From the North Entrance, travel south on North Entrance Road following signs to Rim Village. If entering the park from the west or south, follow Crater Lake Highway to Munson Valley Road and follow signage to Rim Village. The lodge is three miles away.

Rim Drive

OR

Your Must-See Guide

The best way to cover a lot of ground at Crater Lake is by hitting the pavement on Rim Drive—whether by car or motorcycle or on foot. Along the way, you'll find thirty overlooks with plenty of parking where you can take in the showstopping scenery. You can hike along offshoot trails and also ride the rim by bicycle. Twice a year in the late summer, East Rim Drive is closed to cars, which allows cyclists to freely ride twenty-five miles of the road, gaining thirty-five hundred feet of elevation with rest

TAKE A TROLLEY!

If you would rather not experience the Rim Drive in your own car, you can take a trolley. You board the trolley at Rim Village, and a trolley captain drives you around the lake, stopping at significant sites and views. An onboard park ranger also tells you about the history and landscape as you travel, making this ride informational and fun.

stops and side attractions punctuating the course. For a fun family adventure and to keep your hands free for picture-taking, head out on one of the park-operated trolleys to learn about park history on narrated tours while exploring.

There is more than the lake to see, like spectacular geology (ancient pumice desert); evergreen forests; and the curious Wizard Island, a volcano rising from within the lake that resembles a wizard's hat.

Unobstructed visual access to the lake along Rim Drive is by design, and the engineering fete was built precisely for this purpose, earning it a designation on the National Register of Historic Places.

Head to the Watchman Overlook at night to gaze into the cosmos and see why the National Park Service has declared Crater Lake one of the ten starriest national parks. With the naked eye (and long-exposure photography), you can see the Milky Way stretching across the sky reflected on the water.

For a fun family adventure and to keep your hands free for picture-taking, head out on one of the park-operated trolleys to learn about park history on narrated tours while exploring.

Badwater Basin

Your Must-See Guide

Badwater is one of the most popular sites in Death Valley. At two hundred and eighty-two feet below sea level, it is the lowest point in the United States, making it a popular area for those who value collecting stops at superlative locations. From the parking lot, you will venture out into the salt pans—composed of sodium chloride (the salt used to flavor food) and other minerals such as calcite, gypsum, and borax. The first notable stop not far from the parking lot is where you can snap a photo next to the "lowest point" sign before wandering into a bright-white landscape that lies on flatland stretching on seemingly forever. Depending on rain cycles and current weather systems, you might see hexagonal patterns strewn out before you; these have become some of the most famously documented scenes at this bucket list stop. Even without those, and on any given day, the textured landscape sits beneath a stark-white line on the horizon separating the landscape from the Amargosa Range that lies across Death Valley.

Badwater Basin is the largest protected salt flat in the world, and, amazingly, you can blaze your own trail into the illusionary vastness where every color in the spectrum seems to come into clear view. It is easy to get to from the popular Furnace Creek area, which starts right next to the parking lot. The level landscape makes it easy enough for almost anyone to tread upon for a most memorable stop in the park.

YOU CAN BRING A MULE TO WATER...

Stories claim that Badwater Basin got its name when a mule belonging to an early surveyor refused to drink the water there. The water is technically not "bad," however, just really salty.

Park Snapshot

With names like Devil's Golf Course, Badwater Basin, Dante's View, and *Death* cooked right into the park name, you can imagine the foreboding nature of the environment explorers found at Death Valley when they stumbled upon it more than one hundred years ago. It is revered as a land of extremes and superlatives—where you can come face-to-face with the world's hottest environment and visit the lowest point on Earth. At high viewpoints, you can gust with the wind and even see frost and snow during certain times of year. With such extremes come incredible ecological systems that paint their way into the three-million-acre landscape in unimaginable ways—such as providing habitat for the tiny but sturdy pupfish, spurring painted badland landscapes at Artists Palette and Zabriskie Point (two favorite spots for photographers), and carving sand dunes that are reminiscent of the most well-known deserts on every continent.

• WHAT •

The lowest geographical point in North America, where salt flats span nearly two hundred square miles.

• WHERE •

The south-central area of the park near Furnace Creek, one of the main thoroughfares in Death Valley.

• WHEN TO VISIT •

Mid-March to late May brings temperate weather and is when desert wildflowers are most likely to bloom (depending on winter rains). September through mid-October also has pleasant weather. Temperatures soar from June through August, making exploration difficult, as leaving your car for longer than a few minutes is a challenge.

• HOW TO GET THERE •

From the Death Valley Junction, drive west on Highway 190 for twenty-nine miles before turning left on Badwater Road. Drive fourteen miles until you see signage for the Badwater Basin parking area.

Mesquite Flat Sand Dunes

NV

CA

Your Must-See Guide

Many think that Death Valley is a sea of sand, while in fact only 1 percent of the park's landscape is made up of dune fields. The easiest to get to, the most visited and popular are the Mesquite Flat Sand Dunes, cradled by mountains in every direction. The sand is moved by the minute by prevailing winds that decorate the honey-colored slopes with linear textures and cool patterns that look completely unique during any visit there. There are endless ways to explore them,

and plans are unique to every visitor. If you can find areas away from the crowds, it is photographic gold. In the midday hours, plan for heat, plenty of visitors, playful dune runs with sandboarders joyfully flying down slopes, and long wanders across the soft landscape. In the evening, you can find your spot and enjoy the scenery as the sun sets onto the area. When evenings begin to quiet, they give way to colorful sunsets and starry night skies.

It is both a social and reflective area—with friends gathering to enjoy the view, photographers setting up for their perfect shot, and those wanting to find solitude in the peacefulness of the area.

When visitors have gone, the earth remains. Polygon-cracked clay of an ancient lake bed forms the floor to hold three classifications of dunes in the area: crescent, linear, and star-shaped. On the outskirts, mesquite trees have created large hummocks that provide stable habitats for wildlife.

DON'T MISS THE NEVADA SIDE OF DEATH VALLEY!

A thirty-nine-mile drive from Furnace Creek brings you across the California/Nevada state line to the ghost town of Rhyolite—an abandoned mining town with great photo ops and a fascinating history. On your way back, don't miss the epic long-road shot down Daylight Pass Road (Highway 374).

It is both a social and reflective area—with friends gathering to enjoy the view, photographers setting up for their perfect shot, and those wanting to find solitude in the peacefulness of the area.

Vast sand dunes laid down by surrounding mountains, where travelers hike the dunes, take pictures of the ever-changing landscape, and board down one-hundred-foot-high slopes of sand.

In central Death Valley near Stovepipe Wells, in the east-central area of the park.

October through May, when weather is cooler and crowds are tempered. Dawn and dusk are the best times to visit, when the temps are cooler and the golden light glows on the sand. For photography, plan to head out in the morning before visitor footsteps alter the pure landscape beneath your feet.

Drive on Highway 190 from the Furnace Creek area of the park or from the unpaved Sand Dunes Road.

Wheeler Peak

NV

Your Must-See Guide

Wheeler Peak has some of the most beautiful hiking in the park, with varying terrain on rugged mountains where views onto it are as gorgeous as views that look out from its trails. For those in good shape and fit for high-elevation hiking, a trek to the mountain's high point is a must. The Wheeler Peak Summit Trail is a strenuous, just-over-eight-mile out-and-back hike that challenges your body and mind as you ascend just under three thousand feet to its apex at 13,065 feet. Hiking at high altitude can certainly take your breath away, and so will the views looking upon the Snake Range, Spring Valley, and the states of Nevada and Utah.

If that's not the kind of experience you are after, there are several other ways to enjoy the mountain, from easy nature trails among peaceful pinyon and juniper woodlands, to moderate hikes leading to alpine lakes with wilderness all around you. As many of the trails start from the Wheeler Peak Campground, camping is a popular activity in the area, allowing you to explore at your own pace and enjoy the beautiful surroundings.

While spotting wildlife is always exciting in the wild, this national park entices tree-spotters eager to see the ancient bristlecone pine. This pine is called the world's oldest tree, but, technically speaking, it is the oldest *non-clonal* living thing on the planet. ("Non-clonal" means that an organism does not practice cloning, or asexual reproduction, which means that the bristlecone's

"HALF THE PARK IS AFTER DARK"

When night falls upon Great Basin National Park, some of the starriest skies in the lower forty-eight states unfold across a twinkling canopy in this International Dark Sky Park. On clear, moonless nights, you can spot planets, the Milky Way galaxy, meteor showers, and thousands of glittering stars.

trunk is the same age as its root system.) They have survived for five thousand years atop rocky glacial moraines, weathering the extreme environment in which they grow and resisting erosion—helping them to live on and on.

🛡 Park Snapshot

Great Basin National Park is a microcosm of the Great Basin ecosystem, sprawling across a large portion of the western half of the United States where waters flow inward instead of outward to the sea, allowing diverse plant and animal communities to thrive. The cold-desert environment is shaped by harsh weather and uplift that create the most mountainous state in the contiguous United States. Here, several ecosystems converge—from subterranean cave systems to desert flatlands to the high forest and alpine.

The experience of solitude in this park is matched by the number of experiences there are to enjoy. Anglers, cyclists, horseback riders, cave explorers, and day-trippers find adventure at all turns. Hikers and climbers set off on trails where turquoise lakes and forests dot the path to the ancient bristlecone pine.

• WHAT •

The second-highest mountain in Nevada and part of the South Snake Range—home to many hiking trails, great bird-watching, and the world's oldest tree.

• WHERE •

On the northwest side of the park.

• WHEN TO VISIT •

Weather is warmest and trails are most likely to have minimal snow, if any, from May through September. Above ten thousand feet, snow is possible anytime. Winter is a great time for snow-based exploration on the mountain, though there are road closures and environmental considerations to note when planning your trip.

• HOW TO GET THERE •

Starting on the eastern park boundary on Nevada State Route 488, travel the twelve-mile (one-way paved) Wheeler Peak Scenic Drive until you hit the Wheeler Peak Campground to start a number of hiking adventures.

Hidden Valley Nature Trail

CA

Your Must-See Guide

With sculpted boulders and a desert landscape dotted with Joshua trees, California juniper, yucca, and cacti, this short one-mile loop has become one of the most popular stops in the park, with most visitors hitting the trail at least once during their time there. And with so much to see and do, you can easily fill a half day or full day playing at Hidden Valley. The area's structure is unique, allowing rainwater to collect there, bringing plants to life and providing a healthy habitat for adapted animals and birdlife. The tree-lined path and towering rocks allow for shade along the pathway, which is a perk while hiking along desert trails and is essential for the living ecosystem that thrives here. Rock climbers love this area. If you are not an experienced technical climber, you can still get a taste of the views from above the Hidden Valley while bouldering (climbing over rocks) across sticky stone surfaces. This outing is an easy one; following along a flat trail makes it just as fun for leisure strollers as it is for the adventure set, and it is a wonderful place to take photographs of the natural landscape, especially during the dawn and dusk.

Once a cattle herding trail, and later rumored to serve as a hideout for cattle rustlers who hid cow herds there in the nineteenth century, the area's ranching days are legendary. You can learn about these and other stories about American Indian communities, geological formations, and the biodiversity of the area from interpretive trail markers.

RESPECT THE VALLEY

Hidden Valley is a popular camping area, but note that there are some restrictions such as attaching your tent's line to a Joshua or juniper tree (or any other vegetation in the park).

Park Snapshot

Situated on the western edge of the Colorado Desert, Joshua Tree is known for its fanciful desert landscape and is easily accessible from major cities in both California and Arizona. Standing in all directions are namesake Joshua trees, each with their own unique form, acting as a welcoming committee as you enter the park.

Harder to see but evident all around is the extensive life that resides there—from bighorn sheep and coyotes to migratory birds and colorful desert blooms. Life is able to survive there with access to areas of surface water and from water swept in by summer monsoons that is preserved in seeps and drainages.

Joshua Tree is an epic playground, with well-maintained scenic roads that carry you from one awesome landmark to the next—to climb across sloped geological formations, camp in beautiful landscapes beneath glittering starry night skies, and hike into landscapes that seem as though they were plucked from a child's storybook.

• WHAT •

A popular self-guided loop hike in a scenic landscape filled with large boulders and desert curiosities including the park's namesake Joshua trees.

• WHERE •

In the central area of the western side of the park.

• WHEN TO VISIT •

This is a popular trail all year long. September through May is the most popular time to visit, with milder weather than what you'll find from June through August—though early morning and late afternoon hikes during the summer beat the heat. Wildflowers bloom from March through May.

• HOW TO GET THERE •

Drive eight miles from the West Entrance Station on Park Boulevard to the Oasis Visitor Center, then travel ten miles farther to the trailhead located on a marked spur road.

Cholla Cactus Garden

CA

Your Must-See Guide

Along a short, established quarter-of-a-mile path on the Cholla Cactus Garden Trail, interesting and unusual desert gardens sprawl ten acres outward into the upper Mojave and lower Colorado Deserts. The landscape is dominated by the teddy-bear cholla cactus. In the evening, when the sun starts to set, their spines light aglow from the desert sun, turning the green plants golden. When blooming, bold fuchsia flowers sit within their folds. The cool thing about this destination is that desert blooms appear nearly all year long (at separate times) on brittlebush, jojoba, starvine, desert lavender, and many other cactus and plant species—so you really can't go wrong picking a time to visit. There are sixteen interpretive trail markers along the pathway providing info about the ecosystem, including birds and other creatures you might see there—and being an off-the-beaten-trail area, this gives you a higher chance of sightings, since animals and birds are less likely to shy away from visitors.

This location is beloved by photographers. Sunrise and sunset light casts warm color onto the scenery, creating opportunities to capture colorful landscape scenes with an immense desert backdrop and with unique details of cactus, plants, and flowers that literally glow in the late afternoon sun.

Do not touch the cactus—for your comfort and theirs. "Jumping" cholla break off and attach to foreign objects as a clever method of reproduction by transferring seeds.

CAMPING IN JOSHUA TREE

Pitching a tent in Joshua Tree is one of the most popular ways to experience the park, allowing visitors to turn desert adventures into starry dreams while relaxing fireside beneath the sparkling night sky. There are more than five hundred campsites in the park, and they fill up—reserve in advance.

Sunrise and sunset light casts warm color onto the scenery, creating opportunities to capture colorful landscape scenes with an immense desert backdrop and with unique details of cactus, plants, and flowers that literally glow in the late afternoon sun.

• WHAT •

A unique desert cactus garden along a flat walking trail for easy viewing.

• WHERE •

In the central part of the park as it veers into more remote areas.

• WHEN TO VISIT •

September through May is generally the most favorable time in Joshua Tree, with milder heat than in the height of summer. Spring desert cactus blooms typically occur in March and April—a wonderful time to visit the Cholla Cactus Garden.

• HOW TO GET THERE •

Travel on Park Boulevard a little over four and a half miles from the north entrance of the park and take the junction onto Pinto Basin Road, traveling twelve miles to the trailhead. If traveling from the south entrance of the park (Cottonwood Springs Road), drive just under twenty miles on Pinto Basin Road to the parking area.

Kings Canyon Scenic Byway to Roads End

CA

Your Must-See Guide

The Kings Canyon Scenic Byway delivers fifty miles of road-traveling bliss to Roads End and is a must if auto-touring is on your itinerary—and if it isn't, it should be! This is the only road into the national park's beautiful Sierra Nevada foothills, descending through massive granite canyons with meadow-strewn vistas in all directions as you follow the Kings River.

Starting in Grant Grove, stop at the world's second-largest tree, the General Grant Tree, and take some short hikes to explore the forested area that surrounds it. From there, you will begin your driving descent into the park with the first main overlook ten miles in at Junction View. Panoramas of the canyon give a glimpse of a place that famed naturalist John Muir thought rivaled the magic of Yosemite. As you travel on, there are many cool stops such as the Yucca Point Trail—a popular place to hike and fish where the south and north forks of the Kings River meet—and Boyden Cavern, where you can explore underground.

If you love waterfalls, there are several. Two of the easiest to get to, and they are both stunning, are Grizzly Falls and Roaring River Falls. Zumwalt Meadow might possibly be one of the most peaceful places on Earth, providing a comprehensive look at Kings Canyon from its base along boardwalk and nature trails. End your drive by standing upon Muir Rock to take in river views before hitting trails along several hikes in the area.

BACKCOUNTRY ADVENTURE

Some of the best backpacking there is cuts through the Kings Canyon wilderness. Multiday adventures provide an intimate experience with the Sierra Nevada foothills, whether hiking in from neighboring Sequoia, camping along Rae Lakes Loop Trail, or traversing portions (or all) of the John Muir and Pacific Crest Trails thru-hikes.

Park Snapshot

One of the glorious attributes of Kings Canyon is that it is almost entirely wilderness, allowing an untamed ecosystem to flourish and resulting in some of the most pristine land in the country. This aspect also makes it more of a challenge to explore if you're not hitting the backcountry—but with established trails ranging from easy to strenuous, a fifty-mile scenic roadway leading to the bottom of the canyon, and exquisite scenery, adventurers can be fulfilled in a magnitude of ways.

Kings Canyon National Park is grouped with neighboring Sequoia National Park to form one complex, and it has two sections. The Grant Grove area is most easily accessible, and it is where you can find the world's second-largest tree in a forest of giant sequoias before starting the Kings Canyon Scenic Byway drive into the larger, main area of the park. There, you will find nonstop views, waterfalls, sublime hiking, fascinating geology, and wildlife.

• WHAT •

One of California's premier scenic roadways, featuring beautiful scenery to the bottom of Kings Canyon.

• WHERE •

On the southwestern edge of the park's largest area, bordering Sequoia National Park on the north side.

• WHEN TO VISIT •

The road is open seasonally and is best explored from May through September when weather is warmest and most predictable and when most services and ranger-led activities are available. June through August is a busy time but gives the best chance of snow-free trails and roads.

• HOW TO GET THERE •

Start at the Kings Canyon Visitor Center in Grant Grove Village and travel Highway 180 through the Sequoia National Forest before entering the Kings Canyon section of the park again. Continue until Roads End.

CA

Manzanita Lake Area

Your Must-See Guide

Manzanita Lake is a summer playground and is among the most popular attractions in the park, where hiking, paddling, fishing, and swimming in pristine mountain waters call visitors of all ages to enjoy the wonderful scenery. The largest campground in the park lies to the south of the lake and has cabin rentals and small and group tent sites, and is equipped for RVs and trailers as well. Check for reservation opportunities and requirements to ensure you have your spot lined up.

WINTER AT LASSEN VOLCANIC

During the winter, the park transforms into a winter wonderland where you can hike, snowshoe, cross-country ski, and check out frozen lakes and hydrothermal features steaming from a snowy landscape. There are a few accessible roads available to main areas near the western park entrance, and the visitor center remains open.

From the north shores of the lake, straight-on views of the snowcapped Lassen Peak are often mirrored perfectly in the large freshwater lake. This is a prime scene for photographers wanting to capture one of the most iconic views in the park.

Park rangers lead regular guided tours during the summer, including a popular bird-watching nature walk where you can spot any of two hundred summer bird species that have been documented in the park, including raptors, wading birds, and songbirds.

The historic Loomis Museum reveals a history of the early days of the national park. It also provides visitor information and a park store inside. Outside you can hop on a loop dirt trail that circles the lake, where, from its western shore, Lassen Peak and Chaos Crags are in full view. Across the park highway from the Loomis Museum is the start of a half-mile loop along the interpretive Lily Pond Nature Trail, an easy and flat walking area with diverse plant life, animals, and birds.

Park Snapshot

In Northern California, a turbulent landscape rumbles beneath forests, lakes, meadows, waterfalls, wilderness, and, of course, volcanoes. The heart of the park is the Lassen stratovolcano in the Cascade Range. After a series of small eruptions in 1914, it finally blew its top a year later, forcing rock, trees, and debris miles into surrounding valleys and changing the landscape forever. Today, you can marvel at the beauty that resulted from the catastrophic events of that time.

The park's geothermal areas are a huge draw, featuring geysers, hot springs, steam vents, and other steaming wonders concentrated in the south and west areas. Despite the wild landscape, it is a treasure to explore on foot or by car on a thirty-mile scenic road flanking the west edge. The northeast corner near Butte Lake reveals dramatic landscape where cinder cones, lava beds, and painted dunes color a more remote area of the park.

• WHAT •

Epic lakeside views of Lassen Peak with many recreational opportunities.

• WHERE •

On the northwest edge of the park in the main visitor area.

• WHEN TO VISIT •

June through September has the warmest weather and allows for best access into the park. It is also when most services are available. Nearly all park roads are closed from December through May (and into surrounding months) due to snowfall.

• HOW TO GET THERE •

Starting at the northwest entrance of the park, drive just under four miles to the Manzanita Lake Entrance Station, where you can get information about what to do and see during your time there. If driving from the southwest entrance, travel the Lassen Volcanic National Park Highway just under twenty-five miles to the Loomis Museum and visitor center.

CA

Bumpass Hell

Your Must-See Guide

Bumpass Hell is a sixteen-acre geothermal basin where water boils beneath the ground, surfacing in the form of hot springs, mud pots, fumaroles, and other wonders on a volcanic landscape that cradles every foot passing through the park. It is easy to get to, as it is located just off the main park road connecting the northwest and southwest park entrances. The movement of steam and water dancing through the area makes for an always dynamic scene—where soft earth is

NO MUD BATHS, PLEASE

While hydrotherapy from natural hot springs is a traditional form of therapy, the hydrothermal features at Lassen Volcanic are to be observed only by sight on marked trails. The waters that form them are heated to boiling temperatures that can cause injury, are very acidic, and even if they feel cool to the touch, they can irritate or burn your skin.

stained by acid and minerals, and scalding waters pocket the area. It is unbelievably beautiful and photogenic, especially in the early morning and late afternoon before the sun becomes too hot and bright.

The Bumpass Hell Trail is just over two and a half miles (out and back) and follows established dirt trails and elevated wood boardwalks, though the hike can prove challenging to some due to the eight-thousand-foot elevation (especially if you are coming from sea level).

The namesake of this area is a nineteenth-century cowboy named Kendall Bumpass, credited as one who rediscovered the area. He lost his leg after accidentally stepping through the soft ground and into boiling earth—a cautionary tale for modern-day travelers and a reminder to always stay on-trail. At the pinnacle of the hike is Big Boiler, the largest fumarole in the park and one of the hottest fumaroles on Earth, with temperatures recorded above 325°F!

Bumpass Hell is unbelievably beautiful and photogenic, especially in the early morning and late afternoon before the sun becomes too hot and bright and when there are fewer people there.

The largest geothermal area of the park, exemplifying volcanic activity of the Lassen stratovolcano.

• WHERE •

In the southwest area of the park, near Lake Helen, and accessible only on foot from a trailhead.

• WHEN TO VISIT •

The trail to Bumpass Hell is open from June through October (which is subject to change depending on snowy weather).

• HOW TO GET THERE •

From the southwest entrance of the park, drive past the Kohm Yah-mah-nee Visitor Center and travel six miles to the Bumpass Trailhead Parking lot, where you can set out on your hike. The parking lot often fills up by midmorning, and it can be tough to find a spot so try to head out early or in the early evening.

Reflection Lakes

WA

Your Must-See Guide

If you want to view a picturesque scene where the iconic Mount Rainier stratovolcano is the star of the show, Reflection Lakes is your go-to place. From viewing points near the parking area, the enormous peak rests on top of dense evergreen forests in full view, with Rainier reflecting onto a pristine lake when the weather is clear and calm (and when the peak is without cloud cover created by high-alpine weather systems). Spending a morning there will give you the best opportunity to see Rainier, as systems tend to roll in later in the day.

HIT THE HIGH AREA OF MOUNT RAINIER

Hitting the high-elevation areas of Rainier is on many adventure lovers' life list. To get up there, you can go big and hike the ninety-three-mile Wonderland Trail loop that circumnavigates the subalpine zone, or go all the way, summiting Rainier on the trip of a lifetime.

The lake is surrounded by subalpine meadows where wild grasses and wildflowers during peak bloom color the landscape. Because boating and fishing are not permitted, it is as peaceful to experience as it is gorgeous to look at. Reflection Lakes connects with several trail networks that stretch farther into the park, including the famed Wonderland Trail near the top of Rainier, which descends through Narada Falls and into the area. If simple day hiking is your plan, the Pinnacle Peak Trail (two and a half miles) and the Lakes Trail loop (three miles) are two popular routes.

For those who want to stay at the lake, wandering the setting allows for great photography opportunities, including vast land, high mountains, and details of the natural ecosystem. At the day's end, you can linger to watch the sun go down, which can light Rainier aglow in pink and pale blue when the mountain is visible.

Park Snapshot

Mount Rainier is a mammoth stratovolcano and is the most glaciated peak in the contiguous United States. The national park is its home, and it holds an eternity of other wonderful traits. It is broken up into five main areas: Longmire (southwest), Paradise (southwest), Ohanapecosh (southeast), Sunrise (northeast), Carbon/Mowich (northwest)—and, of course, the high peaks of Rainier, with the summit standing at 14,410 feet. Inside the sprawling environment live ancient forests of Douglas fir, cedar, and western hemlock trees; six major glacier-formed rivers; and subalpine meadows that cradle birdlife and animals.

Rainier is a great adventure park—where outdoor lovers hit the area each season to hike and camp through the backcountry and at established campgrounds, bike the extensive park roads, fish mountain streams, and enjoy winter sports of all kinds. Photographers find joy throughout the extensive wilderness, as do history buffs, who can see some of the oldest park architecture in the system.

• WHAT •

A tranquil subalpine lake setting surrounded by meadows and evergreen forests with views of Mount Rainier in the reflective waters when the weather allows.

• WHERE •

In the south-central area of the park in the Paradise section, south of Mount Rainier.

• WHEN TO VISIT •

Reflection Lakes is open to vehicles from June through September, which is high season in the park. Morning offers the best chance of seeing calm reflections. The area is accessible to hikers and snowshoers heading in on foot the remainder of the year.

• HOW TO GET THERE •

Start at the Henry M. Jackson Memorial Visitor Center and drive three and a half miles south along Stevens Canyon Road, then follow signage to the parking area. Reflection Lakes sits approximately one mile east of Inspiration Point.

Grove of the Patriarchs Trail

WA

Your Must-See Guide

Abundant old-growth forests live throughout the Mount Rainier ecosystem, and one of the best places to get up close to the massive, red-barked trees is along the Grove of the Patriarchs Trail. The one-mile out-and-back path wanders through an evergreen paradise filled with Douglas firs, western red cedars, and western hemlock trees—some of which are a thousand years old and some rising as high as fifty feet skyward. The forest floors are decorated with verdant soil and undergrowth that sprawls out to create a complex ecosystem that couldn't be more peaceful.

There is great variety on this short hike on well-established dirt pathways, boardwalks, and small bridges that cross mountain waterways. In the stone riverbeds, you will discover ancient geology in the form of colorful rocks that are smoothed by the constantly flowing water. At the small suspension bridge, many wander down to the shore that lies beneath it to cool off in the clear mountain water.

There are interpretive trail markers along the way that explain the region and its unique flora and fauna, while birds flit from branch to branch singing in harmony into the canopies. For those who want to experience more than a mile among the century-old trees, there are several trails that connect to this area, including the Eastside Trail and the Silver Falls Trail to form a more extensive network. There is also excellent camping located by the Ohanapecosh Visitor Center, which is open during the summer.

WHILE YOU ARE WAITING

As there is only one person allowed on the suspension bridge at a time, the wait can get long, especially during peak times. While waiting, take time to survey the ancient trees and colorful river rocks lying beneath the crystal clear mountain water.

In the stone riverbeds, you will discover ancient geology in the form of colorful rocks that are smoothed by the constantly flowing water. At the small suspension bridge, many wander down to the shore that lies beneath it to cool off in the clear mountain water.

North Cascades Scenic Byway

WA

Your Must-See Guide

If you only have one day in North Cascades National Park, this scenic drive should be at the top of your list—especially if you are arriving by car. The drive is spectacular, with epic views onto the mountains, evergreen forests, and impossibly colorful alpine lakes.

The North Cascades Highway, once a dirt-road wagon route, is part of the Cascade Loop National Scenic Byway, traveling four hundred and forty miles across the northern part of the state. Thirty miles of

PART OF A NATIONAL PARK COMPLEX

North Cascades National Park joins two adjacent areas, Ross Lake National Recreation Area and Lake Chelan National Recreation Area, to form a National Park Complex—all popular areas that permit motorized watersport (with several restrictions), making it a fun (and busy) spot for watersport during the summer.

the roadway are contained in the national park. Cruising in passenger vehicles, on a motorcycle or biped, or traveling on foot on great backpacking adventures are all popular ways to take in the scenery along one of Washington's most prized scenic roadways. There are also points where you can start off on trails leading into what feels like a perfect alpine wilderness.

Popular stops along the highway reveal some of the best of the national park. The North Cascades Visitor Center provides an opportunity to talk to the rangers, make plans, and get advice while looking at a large topographical relief map that will show you just how huge the wilderness you are exploring really is. Outside, there are accessible interpretive trails for easy strolls among beautiful nature, including the Gorge Creek Falls trail that follows a short path to an overlook to see cascading water below. The undisputed star of the roadway is at overlooks where you can look upon Ross and Diablo

Lakes and gaze at the brilliant waters sparkling in the valley areas below.

Park Snapshot

North Cascades collects many exquisite natural features in one concentrated area in the form of vividly colored alpine lakes, blankets of evergreens, craggy steel-gray peaks, and waterfalls cascading in every direction—hence the name the "North Cascades." It also has more than three hundred glaciers, the most of any park in the contiguous United States.

Glacier-carved mountains fall into valleys where summer wildflowers bloom and into still waters where paddlers float across glass-pure reflections. Old-growth trees fill out dense forests, shading fertile undergrowth that allows life to flourish, including thousands of living species ranging from large mammals, birds, and fish to bioorganic lichen spread across rock faces.

With more than four hundred miles of established trails, this is a premier park for backpacking and hiking. Trails range from short and accessible to all-encompassing expeditions higher into the alpine areas. You may even cross paths with thru-hikers traveling the Pacific Crest Trail.

• WHAT •

A scenic byway popular with Washington residents and travelers alike, crossing through the heart of the national park where alpine views and evergreen forests accompany you the entire way.

• WHERE •

In the central area of the park, cutting east to west.

• WHEN TO VISIT •

The roadway is open from May through the area's first snowfall of the winter season (usually occurring sometime in November). Outside of that time, avalanches in the high mountains can render the highway impassable. Check for road closures before you head in.

• HOW TO GET THERE •

If entering the park from the west, travel on SR 20 (North Cascades Highway) from Interstate 5 at Burlington. Entering from the east, you will meet a rendezvous point with the highway from US Route 97 at Okanogan, or WA 153 at Twisp.

WA

Diablo Lake

Your Must-See Guide

Whether perched on an overlook on the North Cascades Highway, gliding its waters on self-propelled watercraft, or hiking its perimeter, beauty lies in all directions regardless of how you choose to explore Diablo Lake—and this is an area you won't want to miss. The lake is actually a reservoir of the dammed Skagit River, colored by glacier sediment that enters the basins with each trickle of snowmelt coloring it

A DAM TRIO

The creator of Diablo Dam also built two other dams in the area (Gorge and Ross) with the intention that all three would provide power to Seattle. In 1920 when the Diablo Dam was built, the three-hundred-and-eighty-nine-foot dam was the largest in the world and cost around four million dollars to build. In 1936, it started providing hydropower. Today, the three dams provide 20 percent power to Seattle.

turquoise and emerald green—hues befitting the Evergreen State!

Along the North Cascades Highway, stop at the Diablo Lake Overlook at mile marker 131 to take in views and snap photos of the picture-perfect scene. A popular trail skirting the lake is found on the seven-and-a-half-mile out-and-back Diablo Lake Trail for great hiking, walking, and trail running through rocky, tree-lined, and open areas along the Skagit River.

Boating Diablo is a dreamlike way to experience the waterway, which, from viewpoints higher up, will call you to do just that with one glimpse. Kayak and canoe adventures are easy to kick off once you drop your watercraft at one of the designated drop-in points in the national park. Boat-in camping is another cool adventure, allowing you to paddle by day and enjoy the lakeside setting at campsites where stars swirl into the skyscape each night. There are seven established national park campsites;

backcountry permits are required and can be obtained at the North Cascades National Park Wilderness Information Center. The waters are cold, and the conditions can be windy, so prepare and equip yourself before heading in.

Along the North Cascades Highway, stop at the Diablo Lake Overlook at mile marker 131 to take in views and snap photos of the picture-perfect scene.

• WHAT •
A shimmering blue lake/reservoir surrounded by alpine mountains and wilderness with incredible scenery and adventure opportunities.

• WHERE •
In the east-central area of the National Park Complex, bordering Gorge Lake to the west and the Ross Lake National Recreation Area to the east, with dams separating the three.

• WHEN TO VISIT •
July through September, when the weather is best to be on the water and most cruises are operating.

• HOW TO GET THERE •
Drive on North Cascades Highway to the bridge over Gorge Lake and travel for one and a half miles. Turn onto Diablo Dam Road following signs to the North Cascades Environmental Learning Center on the lake's north side. From there, you can find out where to drop your watercraft and set out on popular day cruises.

Hoh Rain Forest

Your Must-See Guide

Some describe it as a world of natural chaos; others, a magical enclave where fairies must exist. However you slice it—the Hoh Rain Forest is a living ecological wonder where an ancient civilization of Sitka spruce, red cedar, big-leaf maple, and western hemlock trees rise hundreds of feet into the air to form a canopy protecting an ecosystem of lush vegetation, root systems, ferns, plants, and other foliage that thrive on the forest floor. Average rainfall rounds out at about one hundred and forty inches annually, feeding the flora and fauna that live in the temperate rainforest. Wildlife thrives in Hoh—some of which you may be likely to see (Roosevelt elk, river otter, birdlife), and some that are harder to spot (black bear, bobcat, and mountain lion).

To experience the forest, you'll do so on foot, and no matter your ability, there are three well-maintained trails to guide you into and out of the forest. The Hall of Mosses Trail and the Spruce Nature Trail are each just under one mile and take you into old-growth forests draped with moss and everything else that's green. The Hoh River Trail is the main trail into Hoh and is relatively flat, with the exception of the last two miles leading to Glacier Meadows, and you can travel it for whatever distance you desire: one mile, five miles, or the full eighteen-and-a-half-mile trek to the Blue Glacier moraine that looks skyward at the tallest peak in the Olympics: Mount Olympus, standing at nearly eight thousand feet.

A DEBATABLE NAME

The origin of the name *Hoh* (pronounced "hoe") comes from the Hoh River, but where that name comes from is debatable. Some say it comes from the Quileute word *ohalet*, which means "fast-moving water." Others say it translates into "man with quarreling wives."

Park Snapshot

An all-in trip to Olympic National Park guarantees a foray into three entirely different environments— temperate rainforests, oceanic coastline, and high alpine mountains.

Washington's Olympic coast protects seventy miles of mixed terrain shoreline where sea stacks and massive pieces of driftwood are shaped and strewn by the icy Pacific Ocean. Rocky tide pools are havens for marine creatures, and beachcombing (and camping) is at its best here. The closest region from the coastal beaches is the park's rainforest areas where coniferous and deciduous forests invite visitors to see precisely why Washington is called the "Evergreen State." The Olympic Mountains lie inland from the coast on the Olympic Peninsula, gaining elevation across rugged terrain into the glacier-capped high alpine region where you will find the range's highest peak: Mount Olympus (7,980 feet). The jeweled high-alpine landscape rises and falls between icy peaks and aquamarine alpine lakes in their contours, and onward across expansive meadows that reveal vibrant wildflower displays each spring.

• WHAT •

One of the largest temperate rainforests in North America, where you'll find a wild, wooded ecosystem and sanctuary blanketed with every color of green along hiking trails.

• WHERE •

The Olympic Peninsula, in the coastal region of the park inland from the Pacific coastline in Western Washington.

• WHEN TO VISIT •

April through December, when the Hoh Rain Forest Visitor Center is open. June through September provides the warmest weather conditions and is the best time to catch sunbeams peeking through the trees, casting a beautiful light on the life there.

• HOW TO GET THERE •

Start at the Hoh Rain Forest Visitor Center and head ten miles west to the trailhead at the end of the Upper Hoh Road, where you can park and set out on the trail.

WA

Coastal Beaches

Your Must-See Guide

The Olympic coastline is a beloved treasure of nature lovers exploring the Pacific Northwest, entering the heart of the salty marine environment where seagulls soar in the coastal air. The prominent features many first make note of are large carved sea stacks that stand strong and tall offshore and massive pieces of seaside driftwood that remind you that gigantic forests are crawling alongside the shores. As you wade the cold waters, smaller details emerge, such as stones smoothed by the force of the world's largest ocean collecting at your feet—where in the shallow waters, tide pools provide habitat for sea stars, shellfish, crustaceans, urchin, and anemone that cling to algae and are revealed when the tide rolls out.

There are seventy-three miles of coastline to explore, with a handful of beaches being the most popular access points for overnight camping (there are twenty-three wilderness camping spots available by reservation), access to hiking trails, and day-use areas where casual visitors wander and play. Kalaloch is the sandiest beach; Lake Ozette is a popular coastal access point (three miles from shore); and Rialto, Mora, and Ruby Beaches are the most popular areas, with huge beaches and miles upon miles to explore. Camping right on the beach is a great way to turn a day trip into an overnight or multiday adventure, allowing you to relax peacefully beneath the stars after days of adventure, with lullabies of a crashing Pacific Ocean rocking you to sleep before greeting you in the tranquil morning.

MIND THE TIDES

When paying a visit to Washington's coastal beaches, bring a tide table and learn how to use it before arriving. Low tide provides broader shores to walk along and is when you can see marine wildlife in the tide pools offshore. High tide can alter your camping location.

In the shallow waters, tide pools provide habitat for sea stars, shellfish, crustaceans, urchin, and anemone that cling to algae and are revealed when the tide rolls out.

• WHAT •

A collection of beaches with diverse coastal environments that include sandy and rocky shorelines, stone formations in the waters, and tide pools where you can see marine life during low tide.

• WHERE •

On the western edge of the national park along the beaches lining the Pacific coast.

• WHEN TO VISIT •

May through September has the most services and ranger-led activities. The weather is warmest in July and August.

• HOW TO GET THERE •

The nearby town of Forks has a vibrant local community and services, and is a great jumping-off point to the coastal beaches. The main park visitor center is in the town of Port Angeles, located on the peninsula on Highway 101 that connects the two areas; with fifty-some miles in between.

High Peaks Trail

CA

Your Must-See Guide

There is a wealth of beautiful nature to see in the park just by lacing up your hiking shoes and hitting the trails into the vibrant river valley where the pinnacles decorate the landscape. One of the best trails to experience this wealth is along the just-shy-of-six-mile High Peaks Trail, where sprawling views onto sculpted monoliths, spires, and peaks tower above sycamore, oak, and buckeye trees. Along the way, you may have chance meetings with wildlife that live within the protected parkland. You will see many birds and will most likely catch glimpses of the endangered California condor soaring overhead, a

species that was nearing extinction before reintroduction through a captive breeding program in the park that has allowed them to flourish.

There are several trails branching off from High Peaks Trail that form a larger network, allowing you to modify your adventure to make it longer and more intense, or more leisurely if you are keen to take it easy. The High Peaks Trail to the Bear Gulch Loop Trail is a great extension along an eight-mile route climbing to 2,125 feet that brings you to the top of the pinnacles. The Bear Gulch Trail that starts at the trailhead brings you more easily into an area where you can still enjoy the pinnacles and talus caves before reaching a reservoir that is a fantastic place to picnic. If you are lucky, you may spot the red-legged frog, a threatened species in the park, or bats that live in the caves.

THE MAGNIFICENT CONDOR

The California condor is the park's signature bird. The condor has a massive nine-foot wingspan and a bald head. Sometimes when they are flying, they have been mistaken for small airplanes.

Park Snapshot

With more than thirty miles of established trails, Pinnacles is a hiker's paradise, leading to pathways that crawl across meadows, along shaded creeks, through talus caves, and among colorful pinnacles that have migrated hundreds of miles from where the volcano that formed them once stood on the San Andreas Fault.

The park is sectioned into East and West Districts, with no driving roads connecting them inside of the park and a two-hour drive between their respective entrance stations. The west side is home to most of the park's talus caves—unusual aboveground caves created by large boulders toppled onto slot canyons. The east side has picturesque pinnacle scenery, a variety of trails, a reservoir, the main park visitor center, and a camping area nestled aside pastoral valleys. Both are adventure playgrounds where day hikers, technical rock climbers, and birders enjoy fun activities in the most peaceful of settings in the Salinas Valley.

• WHAT •

Breathtaking scenery among the park's namesake pinnacle formations, traveling through woodlands to areas where views stretch across the landscape.

• WHERE •

In the central-west area of the park if looking at the map, but on the east side in terms of access.

• WHEN TO VISIT •

September through May has the best weather at Pinnacles, outside of the peak summer window when temperatures can be uncomfortable and even brutal. March through May presents beautiful wildflower displays; September and October are the height of fall foliage.

• HOW TO GET THERE •

Entering the park from the northeast side, drive on CA Highway 25 for just under three miles to the East Side entrance of Pinnacles Visitor Center, then travel just under three miles onward to the Bear Gulch Day Use Area where the trail begins.

Tall Trees Trail

CA

Your Must-See Guide

If you are a lover of trees, the Tall Trees Trail is going to be one of your favorite places—where the planet's tallest trees rise upward from old-growth forests that are drenched in emerald-green vegetation. The tallest tree is named Hyperion, of the *Sequoia sempervirens* species, and its exact location is known only by a select few in an effort to protect it and the surrounding habitat—but you can get close and perhaps even stand right beside it without even knowing. The trail is

a just-over-three-mile loop but is noted as moderately strenuous due to its steep grades. After hiking over one mile, you will meet an offshoot trail where the magical forest comes to life in a secret garden where trees, vines, and plants meander across the forest floor with canopies nested above you. The upper canopy is a collection of redwoods, western hemlock, and Douglas firs where flying squirrels and bird species like the rare marbled murrelet can be seen. The middle canopy is filled with tan oak and flowering rhododendrons that shield the ground areas, allowing wildlife to travel quietly through the area. The forest floor is a commingling of fallen trees and stone-laden soil, ferns and mosses, and seemingly every dynamic form of vegetation that you might imagine in an old-growth forest.

After a few hours of exploring, you might forget your initial quest of seeing tall trees—of which you can never really see the tops of—as you marvel at the dynamic ecosystem.

PLAN AHEAD

Redwood is an ever-changing environment, and advance planning will help improve your time there. Head to one of the visitor centers to check for closures and learn which areas require permits. Note that GPS is often inaccurate when plotting destinations. Download the National Park Service app before your trip.

Park Snapshot

From the inland forest to the Pacific coast, Redwood sprawls out across national and state parkland, protecting an enchanting ecosystem of woodlands, wild rivers, and healthy vegetation. Animals like bear, deer, and several herds of Roosevelt elk (the only place they live in California) roam peacefully. One-third of the bird species documented in the United States have been recorded in the park's streams and canopies of old-growth and second-growth conifer forests. Every year when the native rhododendron trees bloom (mid-May through early June), pops of color burst in the wooded areas with glorious blooms. Well-mapped scenic driving roads bring you through it all and stop at various trailheads throughout the park where you can wander into the forested environment. Forty miles of coastline serve as a main thoroughfare between areas, where you can capture picturesque views of rocky coastlines and breathe in the salty sea air along the continental coastline.

• WHAT •

A trail winding among the tallest trees on Earth in an old-growth forest.

• WHERE •

In the central area of the park, east of the coast.

• WHEN TO VISIT •

Weather in this park is typically temperate throughout the year. May through September has the least rainfall; June through August is the warmest time.

• HOW TO GET THERE •

To travel this trail, you must stop at one of the park visitor centers to obtain an entrance pass and a gate combination. To reach the trailhead, exit Redwood Highway in the coastal area of the park onto Bald Hills Road until you reach the Tall Trees access road. After entering through the gate, head six miles down the relatively well-maintained dirt road to the trailhead.

Fern Canyon

Your Must-See Guide

Old-growth forests in Northern California are known for beautiful greenery, and at Fern Canyon, you can see immaculate displays of vegetation on fifty-foot walls, where nearly ten species of ancient ferns hug the walls and cascade throughout the area. The environment immediately calls to mind scenes from movies, of which several have been filmed here, and the location is photogenic beyond imagination.

Along the lollipop loop and short one-mile hike with little elevation gain, you will find beauty of all kinds while sidestepping, or stepping over, downed trees along smoothed river rock the entire way. During high season, wooden footbridges are installed to help travelers explore the area without getting their feet wet—but if you are into traversing the river line, you can do so to your heart's content. Birds, insects, and amphibians making home in the lush habitat bring nature songs to the water-rich and biodiverse environment. There are no intersecting trail networks, which allows you to focus on your journey, and few other hikers, making for an intimate experience. You'll want to keep your eyes wide open for Roosevelt elk—they are as majestic as they are protective of their herds, especially with their young in tow. Wear waterproof hiking shoes or water shoes with good traction, and layer up so that you are prepared for the varying nature of the environment (and bring dry shoes to slip into at the end of your hike).

ELK SAFETY

Roosevelt elk should not be approached for any reason. Females have been known to protect their young by rearing up and kicking at the human head and male elk fighting for dominance are often defensive and aggressive and have huge antlers that can be deadly. Be respectful and keep your distance from these stately but sometimes hazardous animals.

Birds, insects, and amphibians making home in the lush habitat bring nature songs to the water-rich and biodiverse environment.

• WHAT •

A popular canyon hike with river walking and fern-covered walls in an old-growth forest.

• WHERE •

Between the northern edge and southern area of Redwood National Park in the adjoining complex at Prairie Creek Redwoods State Park.

• WHEN TO VISIT •

June through September is the warmest time, with low water flow making water crossings easier. Other times of the year are still great but have more precipitation, so layer up and bring your water gear.

• HOW TO GET THERE •

Reach Fern Canyon off Highway 101 at Orick traveling onto Davidson Road (unpaved and with stream crossings) for ten miles to the parking area (permit required). You can also hike eleven miles (round trip) to Fern Canyon from the Prairie Creek Visitor Center (no permit needed).

General Sherman Tree

CA

Your Must-See Guide

This national park's most famous feature is the General Sherman sequoia tree, the largest tree on Earth by volume, and a can't-miss sight when traveling to Sequoia! The tree started growing in the Giant Forest more than twenty-two hundred years ago and stands two hundred and seventy-five feet tall today with a thirty-six-foot base in diameter—all perspectives that are challenging to wrap your arms around when standing against the behemoth tree.

HISTORICAL SCENES IN CRESCENT MEADOW

History is felt in America's second national park at curious points of interest in and near Crescent Meadow. Check out Tharp's Log, a hollowed-out tree carved by the first non-native resident of the forest, and Tunnel Log, a fallen sequoia crossing the roadway with a hole cut just large enough to drive through.

Your journey to reach the General Sherman Tree is every bit as mesmerizing as the main attraction is. You will enter a forest that makes you feel as though you are in a parallel universe—where the trunks are so enormous, the bark so colorful, the roots far reaching, and the soil so rich that you are completely engulfed and cannot see anything else nearby.

The trail from the parking area is less than a mile away. To reach it, you will descend a moderately steep section, which you will also climb back up when you return to the lot. Along the way, learning about the majestic sequoia trees and natural history of the environment is made easy with interpretive markers positioned on the trail.

Forest fires in the area have threatened the Giant Forest and General Sherman Tree in recent years, and while these trees are resistant to fire with their insulated bark, the area remains threatened. You may see protective aluminum wrapping around the base of the tree during your visit—a method of protection instituted by the Park Service, firefighters, and the US Forest Service.

 Park Snapshot

Sequoia National Park shares a boundary with Kings Canyon National Park along a continuum of ecosystems cutting through the Sierra Nevada mountain range. Elevations range from thirteen hundred feet to the tallest peak in the lower forty-eight states: Mount Whitney, topping out at 14,494 feet. Together with its neighboring park, this area is called the "Land of Giants"— where deep, dark forests of pine, fir, and cedar trees give way to sky-high redwoods and the largest trees on the planet, the sequoia. The park hosts endless natural draws beyond the big trees, from granite stone formations that stand into the clouds to marble caverns belowground. In the foothills at lower elevations, lush valleys, grasslands, and river valleys bring the mountain and subterranean ecosystems together and is where abundant wildlife species thrive in the shadow of the towering landscape.

• WHAT •

The world's largest tree by volume, nestled in a forest of massive sequoias and other big trees.

• WHERE •

In the northwestern area of the park, between the Lodgepole and Foothills Visitor Centers.

• WHEN TO VISIT •

May through September, when the trail is typically free of ice and snow.

• HOW TO GET THERE •

From the Giant Forest Museum, drive north on Generals Highway following well-marked signage to the parking lot for disabled visitors on the right side. If heading to the main trail, take the turnoff onto Wolverton Road, which is just beyond that lot and leads to the main trailhead parking area. Parking can be a challenge at this popular spot. Shuttles operated by the National Park Service are available during the summer season and run frequently.

Moro Rock

Your Must-See Guide

Moro Rock is a visitor favorite at Sequoia, whether you are viewing its striking granite dome from the peaks and valleys beneath it or standing on its edge catching a view of the San Joaquin Valley on one side and a sprawling wilderness on the other.

The smoothed-stone rock face is one of the first national park landmarks cultivated after the Giant Forest was established more than a hundred years ago. The trail onto it ascends three hundred and fifty steps up a staircase carved in the

SOME CAVEATS

The trail up Moro Rock has no junctions and is only wide enough for one hiker in several spots. Although there are handrails, it is recommended that you take small children by the hand, as some of the drop-offs are steep. And remember, if you have a fear of heights, crossing some of the ledges may be too much for you depending on your tolerance.

earth. You will travel established trails protected by guide rails along steep edges that lead to bigger and greater views the farther you go. Looking ahead, the Great Western Divide of the Sierra Nevada range sprawls out before you in the distance. Looking down, the Kaweah River and Generals Highway look tiny sitting thousands of feet below. At the end of the trail, there are 360-degree views of flawless skyway, mountains, and wilderness vistas where on a clear day it feels like you can see the world!

If you fear heights or exposure, hiking the full trail may not be for you, as there are steep drops the entire way—but don't let that deter you from exploring at least some of the trail. You can still get a taste of the scenery and geology while standing in the clouds on early sections of the trail.

Unexpected weather patterns may cause closures, so check with the Park Service rangers in advance of your visit and plan ahead.

You will travel established trails protected by guide rails along steep edges that lead to bigger and greater views the farther you go. Looking ahead, the Great Western Divide of the Sierra Nevada range sprawls out before you in the distance.

• WHAT •

A granite rock dome with trail access onto it leading to spectacular panoramic views.

• WHERE •

In the northwest area of the park near the Giant Forest Museum.

• WHEN TO VISIT •

May through October has the best weather in the area, with July and August being the busiest months on the trail. The Moro Rock Trail is closed during winter for visitor safety.

• HOW TO GET THERE •

Drive the Generals Highway from the Lodgepole Visitor Center (north) or the Foothills Visitor Center (south), following signage to the Giant Forest Museum one mile from the Moro Rock parking area. Free park-operated shuttles are available throughout the summer between the Giant Forest Museum and Moro Rock and provide the only vehicle access to the parking lot during busy high-season weekends.

Tunnel View

CA

Your Must-See Guide

If you have ever wondered if Yosemite is as beautiful as people describe, a stop at Tunnel View will answer that question. Yes, it is!—and it may be one of the most enchanting places on Earth. The view from the lookout is one of the most breathtaking scenes imaginable and often brings tears to people's eyes. The whole of the scene is a triumphant symphony of nature's most beautiful features wrapped into one sprawling area.

There is so much to look at that it is almost hard to comprehend. Sublime granite rock formations such as Half Dome and El Capitan look smooth from this distance but are filled with deep cracks from erosion where technical climbers forge vertical adventures into the sky. Forests of pine, oak, cedar, and fir blanket the landscape, where you can see wildlife roaming with your mind's eye. The valley and its uprising peaks cradle the vast ecosystem of the valley, including Bridalveil Fall, which looks like it is painted into the landscape and cascades all year long.

This stop is a must-see for all visiting Yosemite. The parking areas are busy, and it can be tough to find a spot. Heading there during off-season and early mornings can provide some calm. This is a popular location at sunset, but if you arrive awhile before dusk, you can stake out a front-row seat and enjoy the

A NATIONAL PARK IS BORN

In 1864, in an effort to help stave off commercial exploitation and destruction of the land, conservationists convinced Abraham Lincoln to declare Yosemite Valley and Mariposa Big Tree Grove as a public trust of California. This was the first time in history that the US government protected land for public enjoyment. In 1889, John Muir lobbied to have the vast meadows surrounding Yosemite protected as well. In 1890, an act of Congress created Yosemite National Park.

scenery before last-minute visitors file in behind you.

Park Snapshot

Yosemite is as important to the structure of the National Park Service as it is enthralling to lovers of beauty—and with so much wonder in one area, planning an adventure there can be both fun and daunting. Moonbows, firefalls, and cascading waterfalls all connect to the valley, where meadows filled with grassy sprawls and streams anchor granite stone peaks. Those peaks provide some of the most prized technical routes in the world and have been scaled by some of history's most celebrated climbers. Hikers travel through beautiful scenery on routes through rocky areas and great forests that can be easy, moderate, or ultimate challenges. The valley floor has incredible scenic driving roads leading to many popular spots, such as reflective lakes and waterfalls where you can see wildlife along the way. The valley has many historical landmarks, accommodations, and services that welcome millions of visitors year after year.

• WHAT •

A prized view in Yosemite where you can see towering granite formations and a waterfall cascading into a forested valley landscape.

• WHERE •

On the southwestern edge of the park.

• WHEN TO VISIT •

May and September are great months at Yosemite, when weather is pleasant and crowds are thinner than in midsummer months. The park is typically snow-dusted from October through March, lending beautiful views (though with fewer open trails and services).

• HOW TO GET THERE •

From the park's south entrance, drive just under forty-five minutes until you pass through the Wawona Tunnel, and the viewpoint will be right there. Traveling from other entrances, you will want to head toward Bridalveil Fall and look for markers toward Fresno and Glacier Point until you reach the parking areas for Tunnel View.

Glacier Point

CA

Your Must-See Guide

The view from Glacier Point can be thought of as a wilderness menu from where you can select your next adventure in Yosemite. It is also a perfect place to take in commanding views of one of America's most beloved national parks from above three thousand feet. Half Dome stands strong as a midline focal point, Yosemite Falls cascades into the valley, and the Yosemite high country fans out in all directions, where trail networks wind extensively to other areas of the park.

The viewpoint serves up panoramic scenery that captures some of the best of Yosemite in one glance, with two main lookout points that provide space from crowds that regularly gather there. Beyond the scenery, Glacier Point serves as a resting place for hikers passing through on many trail networks that enter the area. If you are up for a fulfilling and body-burning challenge, a classic Yosemite hike starts from the valley floor up the Four Mile Trail to Glacier Point, where you can rest awhile before continuing along the Panorama Trail back down to the valley floor.

If you want to try a variation of trails that surround and lead off from Glacier Point, a National Park Service shuttle van operates in the area during high season and can drop you off in the morning and pick you up at the end of the day.

YOSEMITE'S NATURAL AND STORIED "FIREFALLS"

Each February, a natural "firefall" occurs when Horsetail Fall is illuminated by the setting sun in deep orange color that resembles falling fire on the granite rock. In the late 1800s, James McCauley, the owner of the Glacier Point Mountain House Hotel, bedazzled visitors by building roaring bonfires on the edge of Glacier Point before pushing the embers off the cliff – letting "the fire fall."

If Glacier Point is your primary destination, endless hours can be filled with bird-watching, taking pictures, strolling in the wooded perimeter, and catching epic star fields at night.

Glacier Point serves up panoramic scenery that captures some of the best of Yosemite in one glance, with two main lookout points that provide space from crowds that regularly gather there.

• WHAT •

A sprawling viewpoint onto the dramatic landscape of the Yosemite Valley and high country, Half Dome, and Yosemite Falls.

• WHERE •

In the south-central area of the park, near the Valley Visitor Center and Theater.

• WHEN TO VISIT •

Late May through October is the best time to visit Glacier Point; seasonal closures occur outside this time frame. The road to Glacier Point closes during the winter.

• HOW TO GET THERE •

To travel to Glacier Point by car, follow Wawona Road (the continuation of Highway 41) from either Wawona or the Yosemite Valley floor until you reach the turnoff to Glacier Point Road at the Chinquapin intersection after thirteen miles. There are multiple trails that lead to the viewpoint that can be reached on foot.

Southeast Region

Stiltsville

FL

Your Must-See Guide

There is no place in the US national parks like Stiltsville. It is a truly iconic and special site steeped in legend and lore.

Standing on stilts and strewn across the water, the colorful abandoned houses that make up Stiltsville sit on glittering waters that are as vibrant as the community that once shored up there. Today, it looks like a convergence of a small town and a buried treasure at sea.

The waterways where they sit have been traveled by explorers,

USE CONCESSIONAIRE-OPERATED EXCURSIONS

With most of the national park residing underwater, you will need a sea vessel to really get into it. You can rent and operate a powered or self-propelled watercraft and head out on your own, or enlist concessionaire tours for cruising, historical tours, and paddling and snorkeling adventures.

mariners, and pirates from all over the world, yet the early twentieth-century history of the area remains the most-talked-about era. The first of the twenty-seven houses was built in 1933 by a local fisherman named "Crawfish" Eddie Walker, followed by others who built additional houses and turned the area into a hotbed for alcohol smuggling during the Prohibition era, with handy stopovers between the Bahamas and the mainland. The end of Prohibition caused embarkation from the area (and this story is worthy of independent research because it is fascinating). The 1950s brought an age of decadence to Stiltsville in the form of exclusive parties at sea, illegal gambling, and legal drinking, and it was a hot spot for the wealthy and powerful.

Only seven houses remain today; the rest were destroyed by intense tropical weather systems and fires. All are managed by the National Park Service in partnership with original deed owners, who can visit on weekends but cannot make any changes to the historic properties.

 Park Snapshot

Biscayne National Park preserves a large swath of ecologically important underwater and coastal resources on Biscayne Bay and its offshore barrier reefs. It is one of the least-accessible parks in the system because 95 percent of it exists entirely underwater. The oceanic ecosystem creates a habitat that allows marine life and coral reef systems to flourish beneath the surface, while tropical mangrove forests line the shore, serving as crucial habitats for animals, birds, and other creatures that live somewhere between the land and the sea. The Dante Fascell Visitor Center is the best first stop for planning your time in the park, with rangers on hand to help guide you to sights in the Outer Keys like the lighthouse on Boca Chita Key. They can also tell you how to head off on paddle and snorkel excursions from the shores of Convoy Point on the perimeter of the park's home base.

• WHAT •

A collection of historical stilt-raised houses jutting out from national park–protected waters.

• WHERE •

On the northern edge of Biscayne National Park, near Key Biscayne (nearest the south shores of Miami).

• WHEN TO VISIT •

March through June is the most popular time of year, when summer thunderstorms and mosquitos are less likely to interfere with your plans and comfort. If your interest lies in underwater experiences, clear waters are most prevalent between May and September.

• HOW TO GET THERE •

Hop on a guided tour with the Biscayne National Park Institute, a nonprofit organization operating outings in the national park. Concessionaire-operated excursions to Stiltsville jump off from the shores of Miami and can be arranged in the park visitor center or through its website.

Boardwalk Loop

SC

Your Must-See Guide

A visit to the Boardwalk Loop is an easy and fun way to get a taste of the Congaree wilderness before heading deeper into the park, if that is on your itinerary. If you only have a short amount of time, this excursion will leave you with a greater understanding of the diverse ecosystem.

The elevated wooden trail travels almost two and a half miles from the back of the park visitor center and six feet aboveground through an old-growth forest and

THIS IS NOT A SWAMP!

Congaree lies on a dynamic river floodplain where waters from the Congaree and Wateree Rivers, along with rains from surrounding states, carry nutrients and sediments into the forest, rejuvenating all life there and allowing it to sustain while creating a healthy habitat for birds, amphibians, fish, reptiles, insects, and mammals.

its surrounding waterways. At the halfway point, you will encounter a marker for the Weston Lake Loop Trail (and a broader network), which adds just over two more miles to the route along flat dirt trails. This extension brings you to awesome views of Weston Lake and deeper into the hardwoods, where you have greater chances of seeing wildlife that often shy away from busier areas on the main loop. If you choose to stay on the main loop, you will walk among towering cypress trees where fungi and other organisms gather at their trunks and birds flit from branch to branch. Benches are positioned along the way where you can stop and rest and listen to the natural environment at work, which can really bring the area to life.

Winter is a fun time to explore Congaree when the floodplain drenches the boardwalk. Depending on the levels, this may bring closures, but if they are low enough to keep the trail open, you can pull up your muck boots and wade knee-deep into nature.

Park Snapshot

Congaree is no ordinary forest. It is home to some of the tallest trees in the eastern United States and is the largest tract of old-growth bottomland hardwoods remaining in the country. The cypress trees were once used by native Congaree people to build structures by carving the large trunks into canoes to pass through the area. The higher canopies are made of pine, which enables natural burns that are an essential component of the health of the forest. It is one of the most diverse forests in North America, with twenty-two plant communities living in the park; nearly two hundred documented species of birds; and wildlife such as coyote, bobcat, feral pigs, armadillo, and otters.

The park's protected forest and abundant water make it a prime area to explore for hikers, trail runners, paddlers, campers, birders, and anglers, who can drop a line in permitted fishing areas.

• WHAT •

An easy walking path along a boardwalk trail winding through a cypress tree forest.

• WHERE •

Near the northwest entrance of the national park, outside the park visitor center.

• WHEN TO VISIT •

March through May and September through November are some of the best months to visit in terms of comfortable temperatures, lower humidity, and fewer mosquitos than in summer. November through February is much cooler and is when the entire area is most likely to flood. Check for closures and conditions before your visit.

• HOW TO GET THERE •

The entrance to the park is on Old Bluff Road, where you will find the Harry Hampton Visitor Center and the parking area located one mile in. The Boardwalk Loop is right outside the visitor center.

Fort Jefferson

Your Must-See Guide

While this tropical island has tons of birdlife on land and wonderful tropical marine life in the crystal clear waters offshore, the center-piece of the park is Fort Jefferson. Unless you are really trying, you cannot visit this park without step-ping into the fortress that stakes most of the land on Garden Key. It is the largest brick masonry structure in the Western Hemisphere and is composed of more than sixteen million bricks. It was built to serve as a military base with deepwater

A POWERFUL STRONGHOLD

Fort Jefferson was nearly thirty years in the making, but today it is still unfinished and it was never fully armed. Despite this, the fort served its purpose, protecting the coast and the country. During the Civil War, the fort was also used as a prison, and its most famous prisoner was Dr. Samuel Mudd, the doctor who set the broken leg of John Wilkes Booth.

anchorages to provide safe harbor for ships patrolling the Gulf of Mexico that entered the area to shore up, resupply, rest, and seek refuge from violent storms at sea.

While wandering the expan-sive grounds, a rich history engulfs you as you explore the compound that once served as a Civil War–era prison. There are long corridors passing through more than two thousand archways and endless walkways to explore on several floors of the building. From the roofline, you can peer off onto the seascape the way early inhabitants did hundreds of years ago. Along the moat walls, you can wander the perimeter with the waters splashing by your side—an excellent place to capture photographs of the red brick contrasted by the aquamarine seas. You can camp at Garden Key, which is a fun way to enjoy solitude on the island once the day-trippers have come and gone. Ranger-led night tours in the fort are available if you are up for a spooky adventure on the historic grounds.

Park Snapshot

While Fort Jefferson commands a lot of the attention in Dry Tortugas and is arguably the crown jewel of the park, there is wonderful nature to explore outside of it. Whether camping, boating, swimming, snorkeling, diving, or paddling to one of the six perimeter islands, you will find plenty of watersport to enjoy at Dry Tortugas. Less than 1 percent of the national park is on land, and there are shipwrecks, impeccable coral reefs, and seagrass systems that teem with aquatic life that you can explore offshore.

If you choose to camp overnight—a fun and different way to experience this park—you can wander the grounds by day looking for migrating land birds and seabirds before gazing into the starscape overhead at night. There are a handful of six-person campsites that are available on a first come, first served basis.

• WHAT •

A Civil War–era fort, the third-largest in the United States, on a remote island with crystal clear surrounding waterways.

• WHERE •

On the main island of seven islands, in the heart of the protected national parkland in Garden Key.

• WHEN TO VISIT •

May through September, when summer warmth and calmer winds make an adventure on the tropical waters more inviting.

• HOW TO GET THERE •

Travel in from Key West for seventy miles on a two-and-a-half-hour trip aboard the *Yankee Freedom III*, a fast-speed catamaran and the official ferry to the park. The only other way to the park is by floatplane, operated by Seaplane Adventure, the only air transport to the island. Once you are onshore, you cannot miss Fort Jefferson!

Main Park Road

FL

Your Must-See Guide

Ironically, one of the best ways to explore southern Florida's land of water is by hitting the pavement by car! Along thirty-eight miles (each way) of scenic roadway, you will meander through a diverse eco-system and habitat along the Main Park Road between the Ernest F. Coe Visitor Center (east) and the Flamingo Visitor Center on Florida Bay (west)—catching cool sightings and lush, wonder-filled landscape the entire way.

You will start near the Ernest F. Coe Visitor Center, the main hub for

PLAN AHEAD AND FACTOR IN DRIVE TIME

There are two visitor centers on the north end and two on the south, and they are not easily connected, so plan to prioritize your trip to be sure you can experience the attributes that mean the most to you. Plan for a bit of driving as you navigate the watery landscape.

park activity and where you can get info, plan your journey, and pick up cool memorabilia from the park store. As you start along your drive, one of the first stops is the Royal Palm area and the short and accessible Anhinga Trail, where you can perch on an elevated board-walk above the marsh and experi-ence the water, grasses, and water and land creatures up close. Cool trails continue along the way among rich habitats of pinelands and hard-wood hammocks in Long Pine Key before reaching the Pa-hay-okee area, which is a visitor favorite with incredible views of a sawgrass prai-rie landscape. If photography is on your activity list, don't miss Paurotis Pond and its reflective waters mir-roring birds wading the shores. From there, you will find more ponds, lakes with boat entrances, stunning mangrove forests, and more wild earth before ending your drive at the Flamingo Campground—a mile past the Flamingo Visitor Center—where you can camp or turn back to see it all, and then some, again!

Park Snapshot

Water is the beating heart of this entire ecosystem, pumping life into every area. The Everglades is an international biosphere reserve, a Wetland of International Importance, and a UNESCO World Heritage Site. With so many accolades, you might think that this is a "look but don't touch" kind of place, but there are endless ways to touch the flowing landscape—from active adventures to cultural and historical exploration.

An easy way to get started is on park-narrated boat trips, where you might see endangered manatees and the American crocodile. On land, accessible trails on level paths and boardwalks (as well as more challenging routes) wind across inland freshwater and hardwood forests teeming with unique animals, amphibians, insects, and birds. Multiday paddle trips are a fun way to immerse yourself as you canoe among endangered mangrove trees to remote islands to camp beneath the stars.

• WHAT •

A two-lane paved scenic drive crossing the southern area of the park through diverse land and water habitats where wildlife and bird-watching are the stars of the show.

• WHERE •

Running east-to-west in the southern area of the park, connecting two visitor centers.

• WHEN TO VISIT •

November through April is the dry season, has the mildest weather and fewest mosquitos, and is the best time of year to see wildlife and migratory birds. It is also the busiest season to visit and will bring more crowds to popular areas.

• HOW TO GET THERE •

Entering from State Road 9336, pass the park entrance sign and travel half a mile to the Ernest F. Coe Visitor Center for information before exploring the park road.

Chartered Tours and Boat Trips   FL

Your Must-See Guide

Whether you head out on a ranger-led tour, arrange for a privately guided adventure, or set off on your own—exploring the park by boat is without a doubt one of the best ways to experience it.

Because of the delicate nature of the fragile Everglades ecosystem, you must travel with authorized outfitters onto the waterways. The good news is there are plenty of them! The www.nps.gov/ever official website for the Everglades has all

AN ECOSYSTEM ALMOST LOST

The early 1900s saw the beginnings of a drainage process to turn much of this wetland area into farmland and buildable land for communities. To stop this destruction of the land and its natural ecosystem, conservationists and scientists lobbied to save the land, and in 1947 Everglades National Park was established. The Everglades is now the largest subtropical wilderness in the United States.

the information to steer you in the right direction.

Park-led scenic boat cruises provide learning opportunities along breezy forays into the protected waters, where aquatic marine life and birdlife abound. They are easy to arrange and depart frequently, making them one of the simplest and most economical ways to see the Everglades. One-day or multiday canoe trips are how the Seminole native communities traveled the waterways long ago, passing from inland waters out to the sea. You can paddle to historical "chickee" structures (elevated decks nestled in the mangrove trees) and pitch a tent before heading out to remote coastal islands with sandy beaches. Perhaps you are an angler wanting to hook a line with snapper or sea trout in the saltwater coastal zone of the Florida Bay and the Ten Thousand Islands. In the brackish and freshwater of tributaries and inland waters, snook and largemouth bass are sought-after species. Want increased speed along your boat trip? Three companies authorized to run airboat tours will fly you across the Everglades waterways—a historic and exciting way to cross the waters!

Park-led scenic boat cruises provide learning opportunities along breezy forays into the protected waters, where aquatic marine life and birdlife abound.

Cades Cove Loop Road   TN   NC

Your Must-See Guide

The heart of the Great Smokies beats with sweeping mountain views, forested slopes covered with blankets of blue smoke, and valleys where wildlife freely roams among historical sites that dot the park landscape. One of the best places to find a convergence of the many park jewels is Cades Cove. The eleven-mile (one-way) loop scenic drive circles the base of a fabled mountain landscape leading to areas where Cherokee once hunted and Europeans later settled, leaving behind one of the most concentrated areas of cultural relics within the national park. On any day of the year, you can wander the road by car to a working grist mill, churches, log houses, and other structures to take in the cultural past. The road is a great area for wildlife watching—with sightings of black bear, coyote, groundhog, skunk, and white-tailed deer among them—which can be seen both by car and when traveling on foot on the many trails that start from the valley. There are short hikes such as the Cades Cove Nature Trail and longer hikes to Abrams Falls, Thunderhead Mountain, and Rocky Top, all of which start along Loop Road.

The Park Service recognizes the value and beauty that the road provides to hikers and bikers, so it has instituted vehicle-free days and time spans during the summer season when the road can be traversed unimpeded by motor vehicles. Check the park website or the visitor center

THE CHEROKEE PEOPLE

The Cherokee people (a branch of the Iroquois Confederacy) in the Great Smokies have called the area home for thousands of years. The Cherokee reservation in North Carolina uniquely welcomes visitors, as tourism brings economic vitality for the community. Learn about their history and present way of life in the southeast area of the Blue Ridge Parkway.

before your time at Cades Cove to note special hours.

 Park Snapshot

Great Smoky Mountain National Park is, year after year, counted as the most visited in the park system, and that is largely due to vehicle passage on the Blue Ridge Parkway that cuts through the Tennessee and North Carolina state line. National park-goers and commuters alike travel the area along one of North America's most beloved scenic roadways that passes through the park. In the surrounding landscape, day hikers and long-distance trekkers navigate complex trail systems that weave through the Appalachian Mountains. Lovers of watersport come from around the globe to paddle the whitewater and still waterways. The Cherokee Nation reservation on the southeast end of the park preserves the presence of the area's native people. Scenic roads in historical areas recant more recent activity and are accentuated by the incredible vastness of forests, where, from views looking overhead, you can see the famed "blue smoke" that hangs over the mountains, peaks, and valleys.

• WHAT •

A scenic drive encircling a valley where wildlife is abundant and cultural sites that describe a settler's past can be found throughout the area.

• WHERE •

On the western side of the park, northwest of the Appalachian National Scenic Trail area.

• WHEN TO VISIT •

Late April through late October is prime time at Cades Cove, with active wildlife, spring wildflowers blooming in the earlier months, and fall foliage colors bursting in autumn. Hiking and biking are best during this time frame.

• HOW TO GET THERE •

The only road to Cades Cove Loop passes from Laurel Creek Road. Most travel from Gatlinburg, passing the Sugarlands Visitor Center onto Little River Road, which leads twenty-five miles to Cades Cove Loop Road where you start the scenic drive.

Clingmans Dome

TN   NC

Your Must-See Guide

The highest point in any national park typically garners attention by providing sweeping views of landscapes that visitors are enthralled by. Atop Clingmans Dome in the Great Smokies, viewers are treated to 360-degree panoramic views of Tennessee and North Carolina.

At the end of the road, there is a visitor center, where you will begin the steep paved trail, climbing more than three hundred feet across a half mile. Atop the observation tower on a clear day, two states

sprawl out in clear view for one hundred miles. When weather systems pour in, you are immersed in the great smoke that often covers the mountains and precipitation that bring the spruce and fir trees and beautiful forests to colorful life.

Along the drive in, there are scenic pullouts where you can drink in views of the mountain and ridgeline until you reach the top at 6,643 feet—astonishingly high in comparison to all other peaks in the eastern US. Trails start and cross through the drive and perimeter of the peak, including the Appalachian Trail, which reaches its highest point at Clingmans Dome. The Forney Ridge Trail leads to Andrews Bald Trail, where you can look over a beautiful landscape on a high-elevation sloped-grass area that is great for hiking and even better for dreamy scenery—especially at sunset. The higher you go, the cooler it gets, so be sure to layer up and wear shoes with good tread so that you are safe and comfortable along your journey.

AN UNWELCOMED IMPORT

When visiting Clingmans Dome, you will notice more than a few dead trees. An insect named the balsam woolly adelgid has been killing many of the fir trees in this area. This pest was introduced to the area on trees imported from other countries. The insect injects the tree with a toxin that kills it, leaving thousands of dead trees in the area.

When weather systems pour in, you are immersed in the great smoke that often covers the mountains and precipitation that bring the spruce and fir trees and beautiful forests to colorful life.

Mammoth Cave

KY

Your Must-See Guide

As you travel belowground and enter Mammoth Cave, you will encounter so much more than dark tunnels and earthly limestone halls enfolding you from all around—but you will see all of that too!

There are more than ten cave tours regularly operating, from wheelchair-accessible pathways in large chambers, to lantern tours that light the cave aglow with every step, to crawling tours that bring you onto your belly to slither through smaller areas. One of the most popular is

A LABYRINTH OF WONDER

Mammoth Cave National Park was established on July 1, 1941, and comprises 52,830 acres of underground wilderness and the world's longest cave system. The caverns were formed by water slowly dissolving carbonite rocks, which in turn created sinkholes, tunnels, and underground rivers.

the Frozen Niagara Tour, where you can get a quick dose of Mammoth Cave in an hour-long trip that is perfect for kids, those with limited mobility, or anyone who isn't keen on confined spaces but still wants to experience the cave. The Domes and Dripstones Tour is a favorite of visitors who can tackle a more difficult area to see stalactites drip from the ceiling and stalagmites form domes across the floor. This tour immerses visitors in the natural science of the evolution of the cave system and the living ecosystem there. The Wild Cave Tour falls at the other end of the spectrum in terms of commitment, where, on a six-hour tour, newly minted cavers head out in small groups with experienced park rangers to explore the cave confines in an adventurous way. Along the way, interesting areas will be noted by cave rangers, such as a cool area where messages, names, and symbols were painted on the ceilings by candle soot long ago.

Park Snapshot

Mammoth Cave is the longest-known cave system on the planet, with more than four hundred miles of mapped passageways. It is still being explored, and additional miles are still being charted. It is also known to have the most abundant number of cave wildlife species that are adapted to living in the dank subterranean environment—from eyeless fish to albino cave shrimp. There are several ways to explore it—whether it be a short introductory trail, a longer guided foray, or an adventurous crawling tour—and whichever way you choose, you will walk through a slice of natural history that has mesmerized all who have entered it since its discovery more than four thousand years ago.

While the heart of this park and the reason for its protection is in the subterranean cave system belowground, there are incredible hiking trails that crawl across the lush aboveground landscape, where the Green and Nolin Rivers course more than thirty miles through the area—a favorite spot for paddling, fishing, and camping.

• WHAT •

The longest-known cave system on Earth.

• WHERE •

In the east-central area, near the main visitor center located near the cave's historic entrance.

• WHEN TO VISIT •

April through October is high season, when there are more services and tours operating and when aboveground hiking is at its best. November through March is a quieter time, and snow and ice may be present. Cave temperatures remain at a consistent 54°F (12°C).

• HOW TO GET THERE •

All cave tours begin at the Mammoth Cave Visitor Center. From the north entrance, follow KY-70, which becomes the Mammoth Cave Parkway and leads directly there. From the south, KY-255 becomes Park City Road, then Mammoth Cave Parkway, where you will turn left and follow it to the visitor center.

Index

TURN YOUR BUCKET LIST TRAVEL PLANS INTO REALITY!

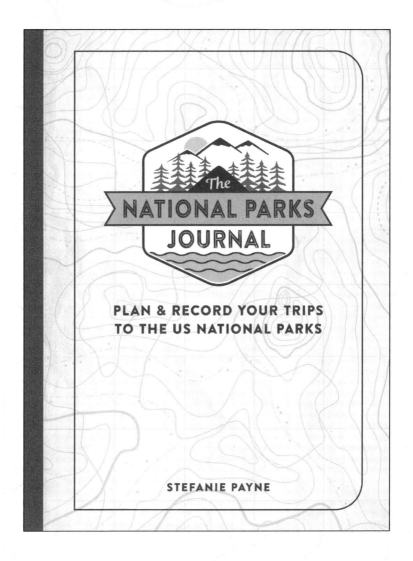

Pick Up Your Copy Today!

About the Author

Stefanie Payne is a strategic communications professional, supporting NASA human spaceflight atthe agency's headquarters in Washington, DC. When not telling the story of exploration in space, she writes about adventures on Earth—with articles and photographs appearing on the Travel Channel; blogs for the *National Geographic Society*, *Thrillist*, and *Lonely Planet*; as well as several books about the US national parks, of which she has traveled the full portfolio. In 2016, she took on The Greatest American Road Trip, exploring and documenting fifty-nine of the US national parks over fifty-two weeks. Learn more at TheGreatestRoadTrip.com.